The Treasure of A New You

Transformation for your heart and soul

by

Catherine Galasso-Vigorito

CGV Enterprises
Branford, CT

Library of Congress
Catalog Card Number: 98-96749

ISBN 1-893284-00-X

Catherine Galasso-Vigorito
CGV Enterprises
PO Box 2192
Branford, CT 06405

email: anewyou@snet.net

To order additional copies, send a check or money order for $12.95 + $3.00 shipping and handling to the above address.

Printed in the United States of America

To

My precious husband

TODD VIGORITO

For

His unwavering support, strength and love.

And to

Our beautiful brand new tiny daughter

LAUREN GRACE

Who still sees angels

I

Dedicate this

Book

"Two roads diverged in a wood, and I…
I took the one less traveled by and that
has made all the difference."
– Robert Frost

With My Love and Appreciation

"Never, never, never, never give up."
- Winston Churchill

I would like to express my love and gratitude to the following people:

First and above all to God my heavenly Father who is always with me and makes my life so beautiful.

To my mother in Heaven, who gave me life and the strength to persevere and follow my dreams and who sowed in me the seeds of caring and loving.

My greatest gratitude I owe to my treasured friend and mentor, Sylvia Jackson. When God sent me a substitute mother He sent me the best. Her faith in God, her wisdom, love and encouragement has made all the difference in my life. God blessed me a hundred fold by giving me someone to guide me in the right path and lead me to the fulfillment of my hearts desire.

The love, support, belief in me so generously given I must thank William Rush, former Publisher and CEO of the New Haven Register, for giving me a chance, and his lovely wife, Ruth.

Journal Register Company, Robert Jelenic, President and Chief Executive Officer and Jean Clifton, Executive Vice President, Chief Financial Officer and Treasurer who have faithfully and in great wisdom given the public what it really needs.

To Rick Sandella, Features Editor of the New Haven Register who never ceases to amaze me with his depths.

Ann Marie Brennan for her insight, prayers and support.

Clear Channel Communications for golden opportunities of working with your company and many more successful years.

David Ives Emerson, my long time trusted friend, who has been a pillar of strength and to his lovely wife, Melissa.

Albert Vigorito for introducing me to your wonderful son and to his wife Carol who has not lost a son but gained another daughter.

With special appreciation to Faith Zila, Raymond Cirmo, Vincent Farricielli, Anna Marie Caso, Vincent Perricone, David White and Frank Galasso.

My heartfelt and many thanks to those wonderful individuals and kind strangers whose reaching out with caring words and kind deeds helped me along the way and to the many readers of my column in newspapers across the country whose letters have inspired me. I am truly blessed and genuinely appreciative of you.

I hope you can read my love for you all between every line.

Introduction

"Delight thyself in the Lord and He will give you the desires of your heart." – Psalm 37:4

My dear friend and mentor, Sylvia Jackson once told me that I am giving others what I need the most. These words ring true from a very wise and special woman... for certainly she is right.

The many joys, the countless struggles, failures and successes of my life have culminated in this book of gleaned wisdom I have desired to share with you. One can not truly write about situations that he or she hasn't experienced.

Through the years, I've found transforming power and strength through inspirational friendships and in the beautiful words of the Bible. I thought if God has helped me so much I'm sure others can benefit from this help as well. And thus, my column... "A New You" was born. And as the Word of God says we should, "Comfort others with the comfort that has comforted you."

That statement sums up my whole desire. I discovered that what made me happiest was to help others, to uplift, encourage and motivate people to be and have the very best that life has to offer.

My prayer is that these columns will inspire, guide and lead you into a closer relationship with the One who said, "All things are possible." With that positive frame of mind you can turn your dreams into realities.

Read, reread and incorporate these ideas in your own life to nourish your soul, enlarge your heart and help you to achieve your dreams. Then get into action. I know wonderful things will begin to happen for you.

Again, remember, with God all things are possible. Persist, dare to imagine and dream big dreams because from my experience, I can say, take this book to heart and you will discover the wondrous "Treasure of A New You."

God Bless You,
Catherine Galasso-Vigorito
October 98

Contents

Enjoy Each Day as a Precious Gift From God

"Untie the ribbons, tear off the wrappings and open up the box. Inside you'll find the greatest gift of all... the next 24 hours you have in front of you."

"Every good perfect gift is from God above." –James 1:17.

Each new day is a precious gift. Untie the ribbons, tear off the wrappings and open up the box. Inside you'll find the greatest gift of all... the next 24 hours you have in front of you. You have been richly blessed with the gift of life.

Life can be a joyous adventure. No need to tackle all of life's problems at once. Take one step at a time. We all have our crosses to bear, but remember, you are alive... You are breathing... That in itself is a reason to rejoice. Who knows what wondrous things you can accomplish today. There is no need to worry if you come up against an occasional setback. God's promotions can often come in the disguise of failure. But, if you trust in Him, God will lead you to the greatest success and an overflow of happiness. God will give you what you want. Have faith. He has wonderful and miraculous plans for you.

Let the fragrance of God breath through you. Don't take your daily life for granted. Be thankful if you have two eyes to see the beauty that surrounds you, two ears to hear the sound of birds or two strong legs to take you to the destination of your choice. Remind yourself of all of your assets.

Learn from the experience of others. Trust your intuition and accept guidance from those who may have greater insight. If a situation is bothering you, deal with it at that time. Do not go day after day worrying about a problem. Your life is too valuable to waste it on worry.

How about your beloved? The one you have chosen to cherish and keep. Sometimes, the ones closest to us are the ones we overlook. Don't forget to acknowledge those attributes in your spouse that caused you to fall in love in the first place. A warm embrace of praise to your loved one can wash away any harshness of the day. A gentle touch, a helping hand and a kind word can let others know that they are loved and appreciated. Spend time with the people who you love and who love you. Take time now to show your affection and be good to each other. Tomorrow is not promised.

So, I tell you, my dear readers, to savor each breath. While your heart still beats, live and be happy! Explore your world, your innermost dreams, and pursue the impossible. You can do it. There are no impossible dreams. Share your heart with others without any thought of reward or payment. Blessings will be showered upon you and a rainbow in glorious colors will follow in your footsteps. Open your beautiful eyes and witness the lovely surroundings that God created... especially for you. Life is your gift from God. What you do with it is your gift to Him.

Faith, Hope and Love

"With God as your partner, nothing shall be impossible for you to attain."

In Ancient times, a ship was anchored by tying it to a rock. This prevented it from going adrift, wandering aimlessly and being lost at sea.

Window shopping, down a quiet and quaint New England street, I admired a uniquely decorated store window. Taking a closer look through the glass, I spotted three little rocks. As my eyes read the words inscribed on these smooth stones a smile came to my lips. An almost unexplainable comfort came to my soul, a happiness to my spirit and joy to my heart, as I looked upon the engravings. In capital letters, the first rock was engraved with the word "faith," the second with "hope" and the third was "love." Three simple words… yet, the fulfillment of all of life's meaning is to have your soul anchored to these three. We could have no real success, no real satisfaction, until every attitude and motivation is founded on these. And the Scripture says, " Now abides faith, hope and love… but the greatest of these is love." –1 Corinthians 13:13.

The definition of faith is "the substance of things hoped for; the evidence of things unseen." Webster defines substance as "the essential nature." And he defines evidence as "proof." You can, by faith, bring forth the substance and the proof that you will achieve your goals and your grandest dream. Faith will do wonders in your life.

Believe and have faith in yourself. God made you in His own image and likeness. Be conscious of your own greatness. Set your sights high and you will be amazed at the results. With God as your partner, nothing shall be impossible for you to attain. That which is impossible with man is possible with God. Faith is like radar that sees through the fog, the storm and even a stone wall.

Hope is "absolute joyful expectation" created by faith in God keeping His promises.

"Delight yourself in the Lord and He will give you the desires of your heart." –Psalm 37:4. When you live your life with hope in your heart, in your mind and in the spirit you have uncovered one of life's most powerful secrets. Hope is never used as, "I hope I pass this test," "I hope I get a promotion." Hope is absolute confidence in knowing you will get your hearts desire. By thinking hopeful thoughts, expressing hopeful words and acting full of hope, there will be nothing you cannot overcome, conquer or accomplish.

Love is God. He never leaves us and He will never fail us. If you feel He has failed your trust, remember, you just don't know the end from the beginning yet. Love has no boundaries; it is limitless. Live with love overflowing in your heart. Practice loving all people. Everyone has lovable qualities even though they may be hidden. Go on a treasure hunt and see the best in everyone. Love one another. In Matthew 5:44-45 it says, "But I say unto you, love your enemies, bless them that curse you, do good to them that hate you, and pray for them which despitefully use you, and persecute you; That you may be the children of your Father which is in heaven, for he makes his sun to rise on the evil and on the good, and sends rain on the just and on the unjust."

Do not judge, just give love unconditionally.

These three precious rocks now sit on my dining room table. In full view, fresh each glorious morning, I tie my heart and my life to faith, hope and love toward God. He is my anchor and He holds this ship through all storms.

A Pollyanna? You Bet, and Glad to be One

"Tragedy will happen to us all in one form or another. A wonderfully positive outlook will not only change you, but will lift up those around you."

Because you have decided to speak positively, encourage others and think upon those things which are good, have you been called a Pollyanna?

Years ago, actress Halley Mills starred in a movie called Pollyanna. The story was about a young girl who moved to the United States from England to live with her aunt. This young girl always looked at the positive side of each situation. She tried to make something good out of every adversity or disappointment. Because of her good nature, others began to scoff at her.

The reason Pollyanna came to the United States to live with her aunt was because her mother and father both died as missionaries in Africa and she was left homeless.

After disaster struck the town in which she lived, the town's people realized how Pollyanna's optimistic attitude was helpful in changing the lives of the people in the entire village. Pollyanna made each person happier and assisted them in seeing just how important living and giving is in life.

I remember a young girl who woke up one sunny, spring day in May. The morning sun beamed through the windows, while the birds chirped joyfully. It was the aurora of a great new day. Suddenly, a cloud came over the house. The young girl's first thought was to go and see her mother who was asleep in the next room. As she walked down the narrow hallway to her mother's bedroom, an uneasy feeling crept over her. An inner voice deep down within her said, "your mother is dead." Frightened and concerned she ran to her mother's room. The girl called out, "Mom! Mom!" No response. Frozen in fear, she cried and pleaded, "Wake up, please wake up." Nothing moved. Not a sound. It was true, it really had happened. In the blink of an eye, life was taken. Mother was dead. One week after the funeral, this young girl had to leave her home.

That could have been the beginning of a pessimistic, bitter and discouraged outlook on life. Instead, I have chosen to use my painful experience to comfort, support and encourage others.

Yes, I am a Pollyanna. It is my choice to look upward. With the help of the good Lord guiding me, I am in control of my own destiny. From every experience a person has, one can grow spiritually. If you have gone through a catastrophe somewhere along the way, you can put your hand out and help another who may have had the same difficulties. Choose to be optimistic and spread the joy of life to others. Tragedy can happen to us all in one form or another, but a wonderfully positive outlook will not only change you, but will lift up those around you.

As you become, "A New You" – a happier, more vibrant and positive individual – you may run up against scoffers that call you a Pollyanna... Then, you can recall my story.

Through the years, because of the obstacles that I have had to overcome, I have become a better, wiser and stronger person, and so can you. Now, dear readers, I can say without hesitation, that I have never been happier than I am right now. I am truly blessed to be able to share with you my life's experiences and there is much more to come.

Today, the sun once again shines in my eyes. In the heavens, my mother is smiling down, knowing that her youngest daughter is happy and being granted the desires of her heart.

Coincidence

"There are no coincidences with God."

Two separate events that are linked by a common occurrence.

"I was just thinking about you, too."

"You read my mind."

"I had my hand on the receiver to call you when you rang."

"Your letter came in the mail… when I needed you so much."

Unbelievable events happening all the time… Fate? Chance? There are no coincidences with God. It's just His perfect timing.

Each and every "coincidence" is really a plan from God telling us that He is in the midst of everything that we do. Things do not happen by pure chance, they happen for a definite reason to let you know that God is in control. He loves you and watches over every minute detail of your life. He will never let you down.

There is such a thing as Divine timing. I like to call it "destiny." When you are in the right place at the right time. These encounters have happened in all of our lives. Mysterious happenings that occur quickly and bring forth new and important directions for our lives. Remember when you almost didn't go to that meeting, but something egged you onward and there you were inspired to begin your dream job. How about when you changed your plans and went somewhere else and met your soulmate. Were these accidental, chance occurrences?

God has a miraculous and wonderful plan for you, an amazing individual with magnificent ability, talent and character. If you have a hunch about a situation, follow that feeling. Usually it is correct. The answers to many of life's questions come from within you. Ask the questions and listen to the answers. Get alone, in a quiet place and pay attention to your inner leading. "I like to listen to music or take a long drive to stimulate my thoughts," says a reader. Use your God-given intuition. Be aware of this power that is built within each of God's children. Be alert and stay in tune to His voice. "And your ears shall hear a word behind you saying, 'This is the way, walk in it.'" –Isaiah 30:21.

Our life is guided by a series of Divine notices. Listen to the advice of a mentor. Be receptive to their suggestions. A soft-spoken word, inspiration from a friend, or the touch of a loved one can help as you walk on the day to day path of life.

British poet Samuel Taylor Coleridge said, "Chance is but the pseudonym of God for those particular cases in which He does not choose to acknowledge openly with His own signature."

Being aware of these occurrences will help you endure and prevail over hardships. Many a time, God challenges us with a subtle happening and sits back and watches how we handle it. Because He has given us this power to choose, during these tests, how we react is so important and often determines the future course of our lives. Use wisdom. Wait until all emotions subside for our destiny lies in the balance.

Is it "chance" that you have read this column today? This meeting between you and I, dear readers? I think not. God has allowed this to face you today, to put you on the right track, to turn you around to Him, to lift you above the world-bound way of thinking. Reminding you that you are His creation, He is your guide and He has plans for you – plans for good success in everything that you do.

Your Inner Voice Will Guide the Way

"I have plans for you,
plans to give you hope and a future."

The Bible says, "The kingdom of God is within you."

God put within me a dream for my future. Sometimes, it seemed a distant dream on a path winding, rough and narrow, with road blocks and obstacles all along the way. Would God give me this dream though, without helping to make it come true? Through many miles of uphill climbs, rocky roads and mountains that at times appeared to be unremovable, I asked, "Lord, have you forgotten me?" Suddenly, a peace washed over my heart and deep within a small, soft voice said, "I have not forgotten you... I have plans for you," it said. "Plans to give you hope and a future."

Since then, I have listened closely to this inner resource and it has never steered me in the wrong direction. By the same quiet voice, my instincts and gut feelings have rescued me dozens of times. And when I listened and trusted those inner resources, favorable results always followed.

Your insight can help you to achieve your goals. Many a time, an individual's belief, strong vision and inner knowledge were motivating factors that led them to success. Learn to listen closely to your inner-self...your destiny lies in the balance. Deep within there is a vast reservoir of untapped power just waiting to be used. Utilize this resource to guide your life confidently in the right direction.

Remain open to ideas that come into your mind. As you spend quiet moments in solitude, great thoughts and creative ideas can flow freely. In this busy world, take time to meditate at the start of the day; slow down and pray. When you pray you have clear insight into your inner self and the product of that makes you a better person. The best inspiration often comes first thing in the morning, before any distractions of the day can come your way. Wake up an hour earlier. Let this be your time to focus clearly on your inner calling.

Live your life based on inner signals. Follow your inward leading. Sharpen your intuition, your inner voice and conscience. Be aware of its power and, though it speaks very softly, the answers are quite clear.

Be careful of people who, with charming ability, undermine your beliefs. If you get an uneasy feeling around them, listen to that inner voice. If it says, "clear out" then run away fast! Sometimes, when we want something very much we ignore the warning signs. But your life is far too valuable to be used by someone or something that doesn't have your best interest at heart. That quiet, little nudge is your best friend.

Surround yourself with creative people. Be like the artists that congregated together in Paris. Their creativity fed each other and produced masterpieces for the world to admire.

Though the charted courses of life can be rough and rocky – with bends, turns and detours – we must thank the Lord for having destined plans for our lives, and trust in Him to make our paths straight. And as Ralph Waldo Emerson wrote, "What lies behind us and what lies before us are small matters compared to what lies within us."

Take a moment now, dear readers, in silence, to hear the whisper of that still, small voice. Close your eyes and listen... listen ... listen... It is telling you that you are precious and each day is a miracle.

Nightwatch

"Besides presenting the greatest matters in life, take the little or trivial things also to God."

Lately, I've been awakening at 3:00 am every morning. Sometimes, the sky is filled with a multitude of bright, shining stars, but most often the soft clouds cover the moon. Gone is the hustle and bustle of the day. Still and silent, the world sleeps.

A friend of mine said, "I think God is calling you to special prayer." And I think she was right. Since then, I have spent those quiet moments with Him so He can pour more of Himself into my heart and strengthen me for the day ahead. Then, I can pass on to you, dear readers, the sweet treasures of His storehouse of wisdom. It is only after I rest in Him that I am able to once again fall into a deep and healing sleep.

In the Old Testament, at 6pm, 9pm, 12 midnight and 3:00 am men turned to God to pray. This was called the "Night watch," a time of communication with God. If you find yourself awakened in the middle of the night, the Bible says, "Do not be anxious about anything, but in everything, by prayer and petition, with thanksgiving, present your requests to God." First I would start with giving thanks. Besides presenting the greatest matters in life, take the little or trivial things also to God. If something keeps you awake at night immediately turn to Him. Search your heart, and if you find something is disturbing your peace of mind, look to the Father and you will be restored to calm. Speak to the Lord about anything that may be troubling you, a trial you may be facing, a business problem, or family issue.

Remember, you are God's masterpiece and your life is your masterpiece. You are a beautiful sculpture molded of the clay of the dust of the earth. If for some reason, it has become marred, just go to God and He will take hold of your heart and remold it again and give you a clean start.

He is the problem solver, the dissolver of doubts and the giver of dreams that can hold the solutions. I have found something that will replace the need of sleeping pills in a hurry. Pick up your Bible to read in bed, it's a fool proof way to conquer insomnia. I believe when we open up the word of God angels crowd near. And when we speak to Him our worries and cares disappear and He gives us songs in the night.

Be patient with God. He is so patient with you, waiting throughout your life for you to understand what great love and forgiveness He has for you. "I remember my mother saying, 'hang in there God is never in a hurry, He is never late and always there.' I find it all so true," says an 85-year-old reader. Eighty-five years is quite enough time to prove God's presence and see the outcome of His loving purpose for you. He is always there any hour of the night or day.

Every individual in the world has their own personality or spirit. In the middle of the day, you can feel the press and jostling of millions of spirits running to and fro after this or that. How peaceful it is when God lets them fall asleep and the night becomes so still. I can almost hear Him sigh a great sigh of relief. Then He bends down and hovers over someone He wants to talk to, someone He loves, someone He wants to reveal the treasures of His heart to.

One of the most glorious things I know of is to wake in the middle of the dark night and hear a single bird singing its heart out to God. Let's imitate nature in the nightwatch and after our requests are known, let us sing our hearts out in praise to a very precious, loving heavenly Father.

Soul Mates

"When the right one comes along, you'll know it"

The Lord God said, "It is not good for man to be alone. I will make a helper suitable for him."

"So the Lord God caused Adam to fall into a deep sleep; and while he was sleeping, He took one of Adam's ribs and closed up the place with flesh. And of the rib, which the Lord God had taken from the man, He made a woman, and brought her unto the man." When Adam saw the woman he said, " This is now bone of my bones, and flesh of my flesh." –Genesis 2.

The ancient Greeks believed that when you were born, your soul divides. As you go through life, you search for the other half of your soul, and when you find each other your hearts recognize, are restored and rejoice. Deep within your soul-mate's eyes, you can see the reflection of yourself. Two individuals are now like one.

My grandmother held the same philosophy. "When the right one comes along, you'll know it," she would say. "It is a feeling that you can't explain," says a reader. "When I met my husband, 24 years ago, inside I knew that was it."

The second greatest source of happiness is a life long marriage to the right person. There is nothing on earth so beautiful as meeting the one true mate God has chosen for you. A new life begins for both when you discover each other… you feel whole and complete. This is the person that you waited and prayed for. This is the one person who will adore and treasure you. Whose kind words, sweet laugh and soft touch can sustain you through the most difficult day. Trials and tests will come, but hold on to the treasure of true love. Things have a way of working themselves out for the good and your relationship will become stronger, richer and fuller after overcoming hardship. Love endures all things. That genuine love will bring hope in despair and comfort you like the warmth of the sun after a cold rain.

If you are entering the realm of marriage, do so not frivolously, but prayerfully. Search within yourself and be absolutely sure you have the right one. Marry not for money, looks or fame. All of these could be lost. Marry only for character. Qualities like absolute trustworthiness, kindness and devotion will outlast any big bank account, fancy car or good looks. In the Bible, King David said, "I would rather dwell in a cave than in a castle with a brawling woman. Examine the person carefully. Get to know them in their own home and natural surroundings. Watch how they treat their family when one of them asks them to do something that they do not want to do. This is how they will treat you. So, look for a person who will respect and support your dreams and who will make a wonderful parent for your children.

Every person wants to find their true mate. Put God first in your life and look for a mate who will do the same. A love based on these things is eternal.

This column has come to you out of the core and depths of my own heart. For God has led me, through all these deep and wondrous steps, to find my own true soul mate. Todd and I will be married this July.

May God bless you, dear readers.

Turning to God Helps You Cope with Hardship

"Rely on He who is greater than all of your worries and fears."

Take heart, dear readers, when you are faced with troubles that are almost too strong to bear. God is watching over you, helping you, and will see you through these difficult times.

Stop now, and turn your heart to Him with eyes of faith. This time of adversity will pass.

The waters that are rough and choppy will once again be calm and clear. Things that once seemed impossible will miraculously become possible. Dishonest, hatred and evil will be washed away, just as the tide rushes over the seashells on the beach. What is left will be the crystal pure, peaceful waters in a shade of sparkling, turquoise blue.

God is in control. Commit yourself to Him. Be thankful for the things that will endure. If your joy only consists in materialistic possessions, then happiness will always be a foot away from your grasp. The things of this world can be taken away with one sweep of God's hand. Have a grateful heart and give thanks for the countless blessings that you possess, the gifts that can not be purchased with money. These are the things that can never be taken away.

Trust in God. We all have troubles. Relying on God can make those burdens less troublesome. The Bible says, "Through sorrow the heart is made better." And know that every mishap contains the seed of its own solution. When the Lord wishes to give you something of great value, how does He go about it? Most of the time He buries it in the center of a big, tough problem, sits back and watches to see how you'll react to it. Do you have what it takes to break the problem apart and find at its center a priceless pearl?

One grows tough mentally and spiritually by putting up strong resistance to hardship and obstacles. Life is difficult for all of us, but isn't that what it's all about; learning to remain spiritually connected and guided as our external challenges arise.

Problems are inherent in the structure of the universe. Never back away and surrender to adversity. It is not what happens to you, it is what you do about what happens. Sometimes, the only way to make people strong is through struggle.

Have high aspirations, even through temporary setbacks. Do what is right and you'll never be bothered by a conscious that keeps you awake at night. Look to God and get to know Him. The closer you get to Him the more heavenly your life will be.

Rely on He who is greater than all of your worries and fears. He is your strength in times of need. God's love is constant and always secure. It will survive even after the rains have entered your life.

He who made the universe will clear your path, move obstacles out of your way, and give you the desires of your heart, because you have delighted yourself in Him.

My Way Home

"The storms of life that come against us will not threaten the stability of a house built on solid rock."

"We live by faith, not by sight." –2 Corinthians 5:7.

I turned to the Lord for help in making a decision. "Build your house," He said. "All will fall into place. Your needs will be met."

So it began, with His blessing, the foundation of our heavenly dwelling was started. A home that will be filled with love peace and joy was being built bit by bit, line upon line, on solid rock. That rock is the word of God. "Therefore, who so ever heareth these sayings of mine and doeth them, I will liken him unto a wise man, which built his house upon a rock; And the rain descended and the floods came and the winds blew and beat upon that house and it fell not… For it was founded upon a rock." –Matthew 7: 24,25.

The storms of life that come against us will not threaten the stability of a house built on solid rock. The downpours, the drought or the freeze will not weaken it. Your house must be built on wisdom, so it will stand and not collapse. You, too, can have this wonderful revelation. You can change your world and create a home as it should be. If you experienced a childhood in a house that was disturbing, you don't have to continue in that fashion. You have an opportunity to build or rebuild your own home.

We must create a home that has hidden strength. It's the dearest place to be. "Home is the definition of God," wrote Emily Dickinson. Our homes can be viewed as "heaven on earth." A safe haven of stability, tranquillity, and happiness. Even your decorations are an expression of yourself, your tastes and love. The Lord wants you to have a happy home. A place filled with laughter, fun and sharing. Family, friends and neighbors coming together in kinship, building warm memories. Let go of harsh noises and confusion and give soft answers. Do not quarrel or find fault with each other. Bring peace and harmony into your home. Little droplets of kindness can smooth over any irritations of the day. A home is a place of give and take. A retreat, a place to rest and to enjoy life's simplest pleasures, so live within your means. Our legacy of love is more valuable than all the money in the world, blessing our children with happiness. Base your home on these principles. Anyone can build a house, but only divine love makes it a home.

Our precious residence is an outward structure and example of our own eternal building. It was brought forth by sacrifice, faith and love. Constructed by human hands, but built by God. His spirit dwells everywhere. From the colorful butterfly on the newly landscaped lawn, to the honey bee buzzing in the clovers. In the kitchen, I hear the sweet birds outside as they sing joyfully flocking to their freshly made nests and two blocks away the church bells ring in perfect harmony. In the dusk of the evening, the glistening stars are sitting prettily in the sky, as a backdrop to the chorus of crickets in the neighborhood. And as the day closes, I can almost see the wings of angels gathering around and protecting its frame.

As I walk though the threshold of our house, my heart is filled with praise to our heavenly Father for helping me to find my way home. Never will I forget my Lord who gave me this priceless gift…built on solid rock.

Include the Lord in your homemaking. Turn to Him, have faith and your prayers for His perfect will shall be answered. He not only grants prayers, but He delivers even more and far greater than you can ever imagine. For in my Father's house are many mansions.

Humble Heart

"In humility consider others better than yourselves. Each of you should look not only to your own interests, but also to the interests of others." –Philippians 2:3,4

Peace and contentment never stops flowing into the heart of the truly humble person.

God gives such grace to the meek and humble individual whose greatest desire is to be of help to others. The person who appears to be the most attentive is usually the most blessed. Modesty inspires confidence and goodwill in others. The Bible says, "He who is greatest among you is the servant of all."

A while ago, I had an appointment to meet and interview a world famous author for an upcoming column and television segment. Driving to his Connecticut residence I wondered, what kind of home this famous man would live in. I imagined a huge mansion, a six car garage, and massive gates. Through the winding tree lined streets, I found his house number on a small white mailbox. As I drove up his long driveway I saw his dwelling. To my surprise, his home was sweet and humble, nestled in the woods, surrounded by God's free flowing nature, birds singing and squirrels playing. I got out of my car, walked to the front of the house and rang the doorbell. The celebrity, and now my friend, answered the door dressed in a comfortable, casual outfit, a warm smile on his face and arms outstretched. I will never forget those wonderful joy filled hours. There I was most impressed with his desire to serve others.

By striving to eliminate hatred, jealousy, and selfishness we can thereby develop a love for all humanity. Don't think ill of anyone. A negative attitude toward your fellow human beings will never bring success. Try to find something to admire in everyone you meet. Sometimes people are caught in a shell that was formed by their childhood. Don't judge the shell, because maybe within that shell is an exquisite pearl. God makes us into new creations, lovely sons and daughters, meant to dwell in the highest of heavens where happiness surrounds the throne of God.

Lets be like a football team, one man has the ball, but all the others run with him, guarding him and following him down the field until the touchdown is made.

"In humility consider others better than yourselves. Each of you should look not only to your own interests, but also to the interests of others." –Philippians 2:3,4.

The really great people don't have to say it or act it. They radiate a goodness and inspiration that comes from within their genuine and caring heart. Enjoy the company of ordinary folks. Only little people act big and attract attention to themselves. It takes a lot of energy for them to always be bragging about their accomplishments and trying to convince others of their importance. Resist the temptation to brag.

Be humble enough to say "thank you" for the amazing and wonderful things in your life. "I have the gift of today," says a reader. "I have a good husband, seven children, eleven grandchildren and good friends."

The secure, confident person never feels the need to impress people with his or her ability, worldly goods or status. When we seek only our own way, we come up short and make a great mistake. Dwight L. Moody said, "Be humble or you'll stumble."

Don't be arrogant. The less you care about seeking all the glory, the more glory you will seem to get. What made Princess Diana so revered? It was not the fact that she was famous or beautiful, but the fact that she, as royalty, humbled herself. And in love she hugged the leper, held the dying and comforted the maimed. Those were the acts that no one can deny made her great. God said, "Love covers a multitude of sins and love never fails."

Take the biblical advice that says, "He that humble himself shall be exalted." God will do it and He is in a position to exalt you to the highest heights and give you your hearts desire.

The Power of Forgiveness

"Forgiveness is freedom and important to our own eternal happiness."

"I forgive you." These may be three of the most important words you'll ever say. Because when you put wrongs behind you, your own life will be transformed.

Peter asked, "Lord, how many times shall I forgive my brother when he sins against me? Up to seven times?" He thought he was being more than generous, until he heard God's answer. "I tell you," the Lord said, "not seven times but seventy times seven." –Matthew 18:21, 22. We can completely destroy the ability of the enemy to hurt us through any person by completely and totally forgiving them… Like we want God to forgive us.

Be the first to forgive a wrongdoing. Forgiveness is freedom and important to our own eternal happiness. Without it, life is governed by an endless cycle of resentment and retaliation. "In suffering, one learns many things," wrote Charles Dickens. "…that it is important not to be responsible for deliberately bringing pain into the lives of others… that without a willingness to forgive those who hurt us, it is not likely that our lives can go on in a meaningful manner." To forgive is a characteristic of a strong individual. Gandhi reminded us that "forgiveness is the virtue of the brave." It is the key to deliverance, personal peace and contentment. It consoles and heals not just one person but all involved.

Letting go of a grudge can be one of the best things you can do for your health. Forgiveness is as good for the body as it is for the soul. Several studies have found that worrying about a wrong-doing has been linked to several health problems ranging from headaches to heart attacks. A deep-seated grudge can eat away at your peace of mind. Nursing a grievance, the kind that you harbor inside, can fester and harm your wellbeing. By forgiving, you short-circuit anger's poisonous power. So begin now to let go of hostility, bitterness and wrath. Replace it with a new beginning and a clean slate.

The Bible says, "forgive us our trespasses… AS we forgive those who trespass against us." Defined in the American Heritage Dictionary the word "as" means; to the same extent or degree; equally. Therefore, if we want to be forgiven, ask God to grant you the grace to forgive others AS we want God to forgive us.

"Don't burn bridges," is a saying that we all have heard that is proven to be so true. You'll be amazed how many times you will cross that same river again.

Forgiveness is a choice freely made. It is a gift we can give or withhold. And when it is offered to us we can accept it or reject it. We can be free or remain in bondage.

There are occasions when we all need to be forgiven. Remember the times you have been forgiven of your faults. How good it is to be trusted again. This may help you be more tolerant of others.

Realize that people make mistakes and try to accept their shortcomings. Focus on and look for the individual's good qualities. Step into the other persons shoes. Try to understand, from their point of view, what makes him or her do the things that makes you angry.

Communicate the problem. Express your concern calmly and honestly with the person involved. Then, look ahead to a clear, bright future and don't bring the situation up again. God has a sea of forgiveness into which He throws all of our sins when we confess them. On the shore of that sea is a sign that says, "No fishing." Forgive and forget.

Forgiveness shows that divine spark within us, for it is love. It is an act of faith and born out of concern for the wellbeing of others stemming from God's love for us. To forgive is one of the highest and most beautiful forms of love. Do not wait to forgive, for by forgiving, you become the master of your fate and the doer of miracles.

Decorating Tips

"From the moment you open up your door, you'll feel a glorious excitement of being home."

I have dreamt for years how I would "one day" decorate my home. During that time, I collected photographs, sifted through decorating magazines and cut out articles that gave me ideas. I even went as far as to draw schetches of rooms, color schemes and furnishings... See, I told you I am a dreamer. Well, dear friends the day is here and I'd like to share with you some tips I have compiled to decorate and create.

Whereever you live at this time, may not be the home of your dreams, but that dwelling does shelter your most beautiful plans and aspirations. Those blueprints in your heart can transform the home you live in now and today. Change is an excellent remedy for that tired feeling.

- The front door says "Welcome". Make a wreath or hang a beautiful basket of flowers on your front door.
- Pick your favorite color and paint the walls. You can decorate on a budget. Look for discount paint. Some paint stores sell gallons of paint for three or four dollars each because it was returned as not the right tint.
- Browse through thrift stores, tag sales and flee markets for one of a kind finds.
- Make your home smell heavenly. Set out bowls of potpourri throughout your house or add scented powder to your vacuum cleaner bag. In the evening, fragrant candles can bring romance to a room.
- Display your cherished collections. On a table or shelf, create a window into the past with a collection of antique photos you love and objects that have sentimental value.

- Rearrange your furniture. Move the table, sofa or the bed in another direction to face a window so you can view the beautiful outdoors.
- Let the flood of natural light pour into you rooms. Put away the heavy curtains and lighten up with swags and valences for your window treatments. Use sheers tied back with wide wire ribboned bows. Make white slip covers or use pretty sheets pinned or tied in place with accent ribbons and bows.
- If you have a fireplace, put a large basket filled with flowers or plants in the opening.
- Lighten and brighten with a color that you love. Choose accent pieces in that color, perhaps in pillows or flowers, and place them in a triangle in your room. For instance, place a pillow on either side of the sofa, and across the room, put flowers on a table. Find pretty plates with the color you have chosen and hang them on the wall.
- If you can, roll-up heavy rugs leaving shiny bare floors that feel nice and cool on bare feet, or put down a straw mat.
- Take clay pots, and paint them in a bright accent color. Plant geraniums in them and put them on the window sill or plant stand.
- Use a glue gun to cover plain white lampshades with interesting fabric.
- Garden furniture is moving indoors. Wicker is an indoor/outdoor favorite. Cover the seat cushions in a flowered chintz and you can create a garden atmosphere year-round.
- Change your heavy oil paintings to light watercolor summer scenes and replace your brass with crystal or silver.
- Buy a guest book for everyone to sign before they leave your home.

The walls of your home will be blessed by your loving touch and tender care.

From the moment you open up your door, you'll feel a glorious excitement of being home. Lets remember the true beauty of a home is a soul filled with thanksgiving and appreciation. Happy Decorating!

The Song of Praise

"Start a 'praise' book. Write down, each day, and express to God something of which you are thankful for."

The birds wake up at the break of day and sing a song of praise before they begin to fill the necessary deeds ahead. They sing their melodies joyfully to God for the precious and glorious morning. And from their praise they gain virtue, power, and energy to face what lies ahead. For the joy of the Lord is their strength. Listen to the heavenly range of sounds, the jubilant orchestration… as the birds sing His praises.

We too, must rejoice in what God has given to us, so that we can have strength for the day. Begin now by saying "thank you" "thank you for this…" and watch your spirit begin to lift. The more you praise Him, the higher you will soar like the eagle far above all earthly cares and worries. The power of the words of the enemy will loose their strength and become like the chatter of chipmunks on the ground. God bathes the tiniest rose with dew and feeds the sparrows. Think of how much more value you are to Him; how much He loves you. Be grateful for the opportunity to be free to praise Him for the special person that you are.

A French proverb tells us that "gratitude creates the heart's memory." Begin to practice this beautiful principal in your life and watch miraculous joys unfold. Gratitude unleashes floods and torrents of happiness that turns what little we have into so much more, as you focus on the abundance of blessings that you have rather than the things that you may be lacking. The praise you give out, God will receive with great joy, and in return, will fill your heart with happiness and strength. This is the true circle of life, so give and receive the very best.

Start a "praise" book. Write down, each day, and express to God something of which you are thankful for. Take inventory now of your life's treasures. "The first wealth is health," said Ralph Waldo Emerson. Express appreciation for your health, your family, a friend, or an acquaintance. Overflow with gratefulness. Notice and give thanks for each day's gifts, big or small. The sight of a sunset, the laughter of a child, and hearing the words "I love you." Count your blessings one by one. Praise Him who created you to be enthralled over a snowflake, twinkling stars, the warmth of home, and food on the table. Thankfulness can turn a simple dinner into a feast, a home into a castle, and an acquaintance into a beloved friend. Your heart will be awakened to the heralding trumpet of transforming power in praise. Praise can be expressed in the form of helping those in need. After a kind and generous deed, ask the recipient to say aloud to God that evening "thank you," because you will be saying "thank you" to God for the joyful opportunity of helping them. God will rejoice from above as you appreciate all that He has given.

A surge of thankfulness comes again in the songs of the birds as they flutter to their nests in the dusk of the evening. End each day as the birds do with a song of praise, and a grateful heart expressing joy, peace, and harmony. You will receive a blessing of benediction, "For so He giveth His beloved sleep." "Sing to the Lord a new song, for He has done marvelous things." –Psalms 98:1. Remember, He created a marvelous you to praise Him.

Influence

"Everyone who accomplishes something extraordinary has had help from someone."

There is a heavenly chain that starts with God, then, hand in hand, heart to heart, it comes down through the universe into time and now dear readers, my hand holds yours.

How many times have you heard these wonderful phrases, "She has influenced my life immensely." "He listened to me and gave me good advice." "I will never forget their kindness, belief in me and understanding." "That unconditional love was just what I needed." "That little one showed me the simplicity of God." "Her inspirational words and caring heart helped me through difficult times." "He gave me a chance." "Her prayers were just what I needed."

Wonderful individuals who have made a difference and who positively influenced my life. Whose encouragement, affection and inspiration spurred me onward toward success and happiness. Many a time, I feel God sends a special person into our lives to be a great influence. He not only created us with a need for people, but He also supplies those wonderful people we need. "Perfume and incense bring joy to the heart and the pleasantness of one's friends springs from his earnest council." –Proverbs 27:9.

Who is influencing your life? Who holds authority over you?

Influence changes a person. Wise advice and counsel can help you see problems in a more rational light. Loving thoughts, sweet words and comfort can affect your entire life. A caring mentors spoken words, their gentle embrace and trusting belief in your ability to make the right decision can become like a road map by which you can navigate your life.

Never let another rob you of your belief in yourself, of achieving your hearts desire or pursuing your dreams. Forget others negative statements. You are far above their hurtful tactics. People who feel inferior have to pretend everything they have is superior to anything that you have. Feel sorry for them. They have little else going for themselves.

"True friends cherish each others hopes. They are kind to each others dreams," wrote Thoreau.

Many successful people today will say, "If it were not for the influence of a very special person I wouldn't be where I am today." Everyone who accomplishes something extraordinary has had help from someone. Their love is the greatest influence.

The American Heritage dictionary defines a mentor as, "A wise and trusted councilor or teacher." Everyone should have a mentor, someone who brings something constructive to your life. It may be a parent, teacher, beloved friend or relative. Young children can discover a persevering work ethic from their parents. Teenagers can master patient self control from a grandparent. A new mother can observe tender caring from an experienced mother. And young men can learn to overcome obstacles and secure achievement from successful business achievers or someone who has impressed the world with their way of life. Draw from others lessons that may profit you.

We learn from observing. Observe the characteristics that you admire in someone else and be influenced to acquire them for yourself.

Share with another the wisdom you have gained through the years. By positively affecting even one other person you can help to make this world a better place for us all.

Do for others what was done for you. Pass it on. The joy you will receive by helping others achieve their dreams will bring great fulfillment into your life.

Read the encouragement of the greatest Friend and Mentor you will ever have. The anchor of God's Word holds your ship through every storm and by holding His hand you can reach down and lift up another.

An Even Balance

"All things work together for the good when you respect the one and only body God has given to you."

Your body is a grand temple, a magnificent creation. Each part working together in unity to help you enjoy every moment of this God-given life. Take care of yourself with intelligence and respect. The care you give your body is one of the most important responsibilities you will ever have. How you perceive your needs directs your actions, thoughts and achievements. So, choose to cherish and honor this sacred dwelling. Provided by God our Father, it is the vehicle He gave us to take us joyfully through this journey called life.

The Bible says, "The Lord loves an even balance." To stay healthy emotionally, spiritually, and physically, we need to have control over our vocation, recreation, and restoration.

- Endorse healthy habits. Nourish your body with wholesome foods and pure, clean water. Engage in a regular fitness routine. Take a brisk walk in the sunlight. Walking is one of the best forms of exercises there is. "It takes a direct dispensation from Heaven to become a walker," wrote Henry David Thoreau. Walk for your spirit and soul, as well as for your physical well being. Stay up to date on your medical exams, check-ups and dental care.
- Spend time alone. Quiet moments in solitude can create times of personal reflection and give restoration to body and soul.

Carve leisure time out of your busy schedule for your own enjoyment. Discuss with your spouse the importance of having time alone, to be your own person and to share your thoughts. You'll be surprised how much more patience you'll have with others after a few hours of peace and solitude.

- Do what makes you personally happy. Try a new sport, plan an exciting vacation or delve into a hobby. Go to the gym or tag-saling with friends. Take dancing lessons with your mate or browse through a bookstore for an interesting novel. Be intellectually stimulated. Continually try to reach higher heights of thought. Communicate with a trusted confidant. And talk out your dreams and aspirations.
- Give yourself a break. Find ways to relax, renew and recharge. Indulge in a "day of beauty" at a local salon. You deserve it! Unwind in a warm bath, an herbal shampoo or a soothing facial. Pamper yourself and feel rejuvenated. Take deep breaths and breath out any stress and negativity.
- Look your best. Confidence will radiate from the inside out when you feel you look great. A sparkle in your eye and humorous thoughts in your mind will convey Joi de Vivre! Buy that pretty scarf or new tie. Dress up for dinner and put candles on the table and listen to classical music. Don't hold back in creating an atmosphere of pure delight.
- Keep spiritually centered. Put God first in your life and thank Him for your blessings. Begin each day in gratitude and express to God your plans for the future. Join a prayer group, read passages from the Bible or sing spiritual songs to brighten your hours. He will send showers of blessings upon you.

Smile and be happy, dear readers. Enjoy the wonderful world God has made for us. "Thou hast created all things and for thy pleasure they are created." –Revelation 4:11.

You can't be so heavenly minded that you are no earthy good… So, lets take extra special care of this God-given temple. Ask the Lord to help you achieve an even balance and peace in both mind and body. All things work together for the good when you respect the one and only body God has given to you. Remember, it's the house of your beautiful soul.

Solitude

"God will alter time for you as you give Him a portion of your day."

In winter, nature utters incredible silence. The enchanting hush of the sleeping weeping willow and the majestic snow laden pines. The presence of God seen within each peaceful and still landscape. Winter's silences have great appeal, especially to the reflective mind. The still and quiet beauty makes one desire to be at such peace with oneself. I love to sit quietly, here at work, with only the sound of my cat, Marla, purring contentedly on my lap and hearing not another sound except that of my own breath. In moments of complete silence, with not a word or whisper, I can reflect on the magnificent grandeur of the universe and the Divine Hand who created it. I consider myself blessed to be a part of all its wonder and splendor.

In a world wind of busyness, take a moment out of your day or night to be in complete silence. The rush of life can be exhausting, so retire often into the sweet and composing silence of God's all sufficiency and be still with Him in the inner harmony of your soul.

When you are quiet and alone, all of creation can open up its wise secrets to you. Ponder on the simple pleasures you have in your life, think about those you love and dwell on the many blessings provided for you with each passing day. In solitude and silence you can examine your heart. What do you feel at its core? Meditate on your hearts truest desires. Look beyond the outer surface of things and witness the divine beauty that reveals itself through the inner reflection of outer blessings.

Use this composed, passive time to be creative with your mind. Creative thinking is wonderful. It can open up a whole new world of interesting thoughts and ideas. Turn off the television, the stereo and the phone. Let the hustle and bustle of the commercial world pass by, as you take time to be in complete silence.

Calmness of the mind is a beautiful quality of character. Look inside yourself in solitude and find the answers to life's questions. Being at peace with one's self and ultimately with the outside world is a treasure beyond measure. Positive, successful living begins with an honest analysis of ourselves and depends largely on how we view ourselves and our circumstances. A peaceful mind generates wisdom, thinking out peaceful solutions and visualizing relaxing scenes. Spend moments on reflection and prayer. God will alter time for you as you give Him a portion of your day. Turn your mind at regular intervals to God and be attuned to His love. You will be comforted because the peace of the Lord surpasses all understanding. Lift your eyes to the heavens and fill your soul with His peace. Problems that seemed insoluble will unravel and the solutions become so apparently simple. Do not act on impulse. Take a deep breath and think things through calmly when things go wrong. Don't ruin all that is sweet and beautiful through explosive tempers. Exercise self-control. Have a calm, yet confident demeanor and spread peace and contentment whereever you go. Develop the exquisite poise of serenity. Miracles don't happen when we're restless. They often come when we are quiet, calm and trusting. Let your mind and soul be at ease.

As God appoints my portion of the day, I try to have regular intervals of absolute silence and solitude. Time alone to ask the questions in my heart and to hear the answers, as His words direct my life and guide my path anew. And, dear readers, I want this so much for you.

Miracles in the Making

"Amid strife or conflict, believe in miracles and expect them to happen."

Einstein once said, "There are only two ways to live your life. One is as though nothing is a miracle. The other is as though everything is a miracle."

Nothing is more real than miracles. Today and each hour of our precious existence, miraculous things are transpiring before our very eyes. Look around your world, dear readers. In the millions of people from all walks of life, have you seen your duplicate? There is superior power that lies within your own unique and wonderful personality. You are a miracle, an original and a one of a kind work of art, greater than a play by Shakespeare, a painting by Rembrandt or an aria by Puccini. These masterpieces were created by famous men. But, you were created by God Himself. So special, so valuable, no one else since your birth was ever as intricately made as you. Appreciate your rarity. You were made for a purpose, God's infinite creation and His wisdom at work to fulfill His great design. As His creation, your potential is limitless. Never listen to those who try to demean you. You are a great treasure, a spectacular human being. Be yourself and shape your destiny by believing in the joy of a miraculous life. You can grow to stupendous heights of achievement.

We are so fortunate to have a loving Father who delights in our happiness. Enjoy the countless proofs the Lord has provided of His miraculous power. A blade of grass is a miracle. Our greatest scientists can not reproduce even one. A budding rose and a warm smile from a friend are day to day miracles that sometimes go unnoticed. Keep your mind aware of the great expressions of the miraculous God around us.

The birth of a baby, a dream realized or the beginning of the work of love… these are marvels too wonderful to explain but felt so sincerely in our hearts. The real miracle is how we perceive the happening. Allow your mind to look only to this higher dimension of life. Amid strife or conflict, believe in miracles and expect them to happen. Take hold of the wonder and enchantment around you. This is the victory of the strong and triumphant.

Look what the good Lord has done for you and I already. We have each experienced incredible events that seem impossible to explain. These amazing gifts are God's wisdom and plans at work for you alone. If something is beneficial for you and is a part of the design that God has laid out for your life, He will put the glorious goal within your reach.

Cause miracles to happen in the lives of others by your actions. Be open to sharing yourself, your love and your blessings without a thought of their return. The miracle can suddenly come forth in the words that you speak, a kind gesture that you do or the contagious sound of your laughter that flows out to encircle others with joy. There is a wonderful source of goodness in the universe. Those who perform these miracles are surrounded by angels, are giving happiness to others and are receiving the greatest fulfillment in life.

In times of need, God will send the joy of His care and protection to overflow in your heart. The Lord's brilliant rainbow light will shine through the deepest darkness. Look to Him. Commit to the Lord. And whatever you do in His name, your plans will succeed. Remember, miracles begin in prayer. God is always as close as a whisper. He watches over His miracles, so it follows as night, the day, He watches over miraculous you!

Hope Angel

"When the voice of hope is in your heart a transformation will begin."

As rain restores the earth after a dry and wilting time, hope restores the spirit.

I stood motionless in the department store looking at the 30 by 24 inch picture. The gold framed lithograph was of two sweet angels nestled together. The picture made me smile. "How lovely," I said to myself. At that time, I lived in a tiny two room apartment, the same dreary space I had occupied for the past nine years. "Someday," I thought, "That beautiful angel picture will hang in my new home." With that vision tucked in my heart, I carried the angel picture to the register, paid for it, brought it back to my small apartment and put it away in a closet.

I had dreamt for years how I would "one day" decorate my new home with cheerful designs and soothing color schemes. I even sketched where the furniture would go and the fireplace. When I would go to the mall with my girl friend Jeannette, I'd show her the floral bathroom ensemble that I liked and even a lovely dining room set that I admired. "Someday, I'll decorate my home with these things," I said. This went on for years!

When the voice of hope is in your heart a transformation will begin. God is faithful to His promises. He will give you the desires of your heart. "The Lord will indeed give what is good…" –Psalm 85:12.

Hope can be defined as, "waiting with certitude." Hope is a confident anticipation of something wonderful happening that has not yet come. Set high goals and do not be frustrated by difficulties or setbacks. The longest journey begins with only one step.

Maybe the odds of us succeeding are overwhelming. And the world may be filled with nay-sayers. But what gets us the victory is hope and sheer perseverance. Persistence pays off and opens the door to success. Hope pushes ahead when it would be easy to quit. Remember the song "High hopes.. he's got high hopes, he's got high in the sky apple pie hopes." Through hope we have joyful expectation that if we hold on, endure and trust in God, we will get through even the darkest times.

History is packed with people who held on to hope, despite the odds. Alexander Graham Bell was laughed to scorn when he began his invention of the telephone. Beethoven composed most of his music during the years of his steadily worsening hearing loss but his greatest composition, The 9th Symphony, was written when he was completely deaf. For he had in his heart the tone of each note. Helen Keller, blind and deaf, graduated with honors and went on to become a world renowned author, lecturer and coveted guest of many presidents of the United States. Keller said, "The world is full of suffering. It is also full of the overcoming of it." Hope regards problems, big or small, as opportunities.

"I once heard a Shaker quote that has remained with me," says a reader. "'Hands to work and hearts to God.' If we all directed our thoughts, hopes and fears to Him, life would seem much simpler."

The next time disappointment threatens a dream of yours, I hope you will remember the story of the "angel picture." It was bought in hope, way before any possibility of a home was evident, and in faith and in trustful love.

Today, that sweet picture hangs in the foyer of my home. The green and burgundy flower bathroom ensemble I looked at so long ago, now adorns my bathroom and last week that lovely and inviting dining room set was delivered. Impossible one may think. But oh no… Nothing is impossible with God. With hope, anchored in our hearts, He brings forth blessings far greater than even some one like me, with limited scopes, can imagine. And so for you dear readers, if you let Him, as He did for me, He will work miracles for you. Just keep the faith, He delights to show Himself faithful.

Behind the Scarecrow

"To fight fear, confront what you are afraid of."

Remember the funny, floppy scarecrows the farmers used to put in their gardens before they started planting their crops, adorned with a big straw hat, plaid shirt and old jeans. As the wind would blow, the arms would move and hopefully the crows would fly away and not eat the crops.

One day a little chipmunk got into the farmers garden and started eating the newly planted peas. Suddenly, a breeze came and the scarecrow's arms flapped in the wind. The chipmunk stopped and ran back a foot or two. The animal looked around, studied the situation, and when all was quiet and still, he began eating the peas again. And once more, with a puff of air, the scarecrow's arm shifted, while the chipmunk stood motionless. This time the animal didn't run away; he canvassed the area. Nothing more happened, so he just went right on around the scarecrow and had himself a feast!

There is much wisdom to be learned from nature. How many times have you started to break free from out of a rut and then something or someone shook you up and stopped you? Get past the fear… that is the secret. For the best things in life are behind the scarecrow.

To gain the good things in life and the greatest achievements, you sometimes have to go through difficult times. Dare to be all that you can be. Get to the feast of life and don't let obstacles get in your way. Do not be afraid or intimidated by the scarecrows – just realize that all they are is a puff of air and go on past them to success.

To fight fear, confront what you are afraid of. "Do the things you fear and the death of fear is certain," said Ralph Waldo Emerson. Ninety percent of the things we fear will never happen. And for those circumstances that do occur, you can handle them all by being tough-minded and remembering that God said, "All things work together for good to those who love God."

Fill your mind with faith. For faith is stronger than fear. Psalm 34:4 says, "I sought the Lord and He heard me, and delivered me from all of my fears." Where there is doubt, replace it with hope. Expect the best and most often positive results will follow because you will get what you expect.

Do not be frightened. Get behind the fear, the insecurities and the worries. There is an unseen enemy who wants you to doubt your God-given talents or intuition. But in that ability is the path to your greatest success. Be courageous. "Courage is the resistance to fear, the mastery of fear, not absence of fear," said Mark Twain.

A few weeks ago we put a bird-feeder in our back yard. The darling blue jays, little sparrows and lovely cardinals came to feed on the seeds and grain. There were also two beautiful morning doves that flew down to the feeder. And then, with a great flurry came six large, black crows… with their raucous caws. We observed, that when the crows came, the other small birds flew away immediately. But, the sweet, gentle gray doves stayed, unafraid, and continued eating. The doves were not intimidated by the big, loud crows. They just continued on enjoying their feast and totally ignored the big menacing birds. Almost instantly, the crows then flopped their wings and left. We stood amazed at the lesson we had just seen. When you find something good in life, don't let anything hinder you. Behind those scarecrows is a feast of a new way of life.

So, let the dove of peace rule your heart. Focus on the goodness in life, your goals and glorious dreams for the future. We've been made more than conquers through Him who loves us.

Angels Move Among Us Every Day

"There are angels among us that many have seen, sent from the heavens to help people here on earth."

The biblical meaning of the word, "Angel" is messenger. They evoke images of comfort, goodness, loveliness, wisdom, and protection. Angels inspire us with awe and wonder. There are angels among us that many have seen, sent from the heavens to help people here on earth. Angels exist primarily for God, work for Him and are directed by Him. Everything angels do centers around God's will, purposes and interests. Wherever angelic intervention is needed to accomplish God's divine plan, it will happen.

Angels can come to us in disguise. Their messages often come in a flow of ideas, solutions to life's problems, or a mysterious stranger that helps us in times of need or despair.

A person is in immediate danger, a car is stalled in a deadly snowstorm, an airplane is lost in the fog or a swimmer is too far from the shore drowning. Emerging from the moment's desperation, comes some form of miraculous rescue. Afterwards, when the victim is safe and free from harm, they turn to give thanks and the rescuer has vanished. There are no tracks in the snow from the tow-truck, no controller in the radio tower that returned the plane to safety or no lifeguard's footprints on the beach.

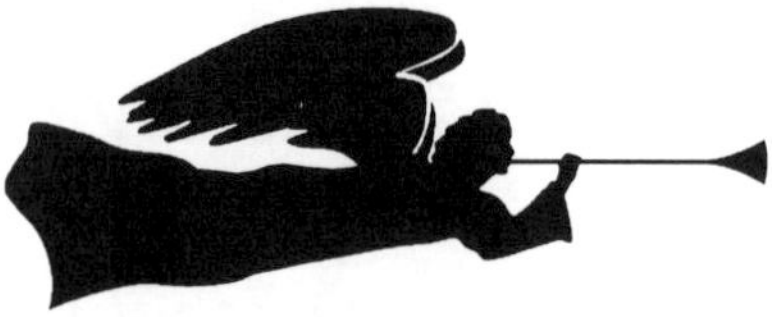

Let the examples of heavenly angel messengers light our paths so we can walk by their examples and be earthly angels to others. And Hebrews 13:2 tells us, "Do not forget to entertain strangers, for by so doing, some people have entertained angels without knowing it."

Many people have done kind things for us at just the right time and become like angel messengers. We have all heard people say, "You're an angel," to let us know that our kind deed was so appreciated. That sweet embrace of love can be found in a neighbor who generously brings dinner to a family that is ill, a teacher who gives us hope and inspiration to young students or a volunteer who unselfishly donates her time. Angels, whether celestial or human, give us reason to believe in the triumph of goodness and make this earth a more heavenly place to be.

Sometimes, in complete silence and pure joy, I can almost hear the choir of angels. And many a time, I seem to see their glistening wings as they gather around true fellowship and on very special occasions.

Outside the window, the day dawns. The morning air is golden and full of hope and expectation. The sun rises and the array of birds sing joyfully. The birds can see the morning shift of angels coming onto the earth for a very busy day of protecting and guiding God's children. May God send an angel your way today.

Soul Food

"Balance your life by feeding your mind with things that are beautiful, positive and character building."

A Chinese proverb tells us, "If there is light in the soul, there will be beauty in the person. If there is beauty in the person, there will be harmony in the house. If there is harmony in the house, there will be order in the nation. If there is order in the nation, there will be peace in the world."

Dwelling in the innermost depth and heart of your being is your soul.

It is there that you can find the hidden secrets of the fountain of youth, the joy of life. Rekindle your spirit, open your heart and nurture your soul with prayer and appreciation for all the good things God has given us.

What particular experiences nourish your soul? What makes your heart happy? One of the most important relationships you'll ever have is the one concerning your soul.

Balance your life by feeding your mind with things that are beautiful, positive and character building. You must put yourself in the presence of the things, experiences and people who nourish you in these realms. Spend time attending to the needs of your soul and make it a priority.

Be alone and be at peace with your own thoughts. Focus on your soul, allow it to express its need to you and listen carefully to the essence of your hearts desire. A sacred withdrawal from the world can give you renewed passion and purpose for life. How beautiful silence is. In a hushed house you can make contact with God's thoughts.

We are exposed to thousands of different messages every day, so be selective of what you watch, read or listen to. Do not take into your subconscious useless nonsense. Uplift your soul with knowledge, wisdom and beauty. Listen to or play inspirational hymns, get in communion with the splendor of nature or the star filled sky to create inner peace and harmony. Before bedtime read something with clean, wholesome humor. Never loose a child's sense of wonder. They appreciate the little things, the soft, gentle landing of a snowflake on your gloved hand grasping its unique pattern before it melts to make way for another.

Pick and choose wisely the company that you keep. Turn gently away from gossip, bitterness and envy. Select your friends with care. Really great friends can nourish your soul. Spend your precious time only with those people and things that you love and receive their positive energy.

Be kinder than you have to, more compassionate and loving. The soul grows when it is giving love to another human being. Studies have found that people who serve others and volunteer their time are healthier and happier people. Look for every opportunity to do something for someone else. Share yourself, your time and talents.

Forgive yourself for past mistakes. We are human and have all made them. Let go of fear, guilt and negativity. Heal old wounds and move on toward a bright future. The soul is made better by sorrow than by laughter.

Have creative outlets. Write a poem, arrange flowers, or paint a picture. Keep a daily journal. Record your hopes, plans and dreams. Reach for the best within yourself because you are extremely important. God made only one you! The soul thrives when we talk to Him about what He wants us to know and do.

Find a deeper spiritual life and feel the presence of God. It is the greatest experience possible to a human life and vital to tending to one's soul. Thereafter, you will be filled with love, warmth and beauty. The soul of one who loves God always delights in His presence, His earth and His word. Turn inward to discover true happiness and peace.

Line up your heart with His and endeavor to obtain a continually rejoicing, creative and always peaceful spirit.

Attitudes Have Everything to do With Happiness

"If you go around saying, I've got a miserable life, God says, I'll show you what a miserable life is... but if you say, I've got a wonderful life, God will show you what a wonderful life is!"

Over God's desk, there is a plaque. It reads, "If you go around saying, I've got a miserable life, God says, I'll show you what a miserable life is... but if you say, I've got a wonderful life, God will show you what a wonderful life is!"

Each sunrise brings us new opportunities to find happiness. How we choose to live our days, in essence, is how we live our entire lives. Optimism can lead you to a lifetime of bliss.

Happy dispositions are created. We are the shaper of our destinies, so be determined to have a happy life. Don't wait for happiness – begin today by greeting the morning with a smile on your lips, a forgiving heart and a prayer of thankfulness. It is "A New You!"

There is a tendency for people to explain feelings of happiness or unhappiness in terms of external events in their lives. The implication is that occurrences determine whether someone is happy or not. But, I think that our own attitudes have far more to do with our happiness level than any external circumstances. True joy and exhilaration are already within you.

To be really happy, live your life following God's laws. It is so simple and easily proven. Have you ever done something wrong, at one time or anothern and were really happy doing it? Did the happiness last? No... But, when you do what is right, then you are on the road to great peace and contentment. Have the right motives and grow in spiritual grace with a God-centered life. The Bible says, "He who rules his own spirit is greater than he who rules a city."

Let the love in your heart flow out to others. There is no greater happiness than in giving. Touch the lives of your fellow human beings with special appreciation, prayers and encouragement. Give people your time. Time is more precious than money or gifts. Whenever you do something kind for another, without thought of return, you'll experience great happiness.

Cope with adversity. View setbacks as challenges. Every one experiences disappointments. When things go wrong, instead of feeling sorry for yourself or giving up, ask yourself, "How can I turn this situation around in my favor?" You have the astounding ability to overcome tough situations. Happiness is larger than adversity.

Choose friends who will contribute to your happiness. Steer clear from nay-sayers and those with negative attitudes. Misery loves company and negative people can subtly force you into their bad moods. Be with people who expect good things to happen.

If something is bothering you, try to improve or correct the situation. If possible, take action. If not, do not torture yourself about events that are out of control. Cultivate a mental attitude of peace and goodwill. Deal with problems, then put them where they belong, in the past.

Review what is important to you each evening. Be grateful for your talents and blessings. Put positive thoughts in the foreground of your consciousness. Going to bed thanking God can allow you to awaken from a restful nights sleep with a bright and sunny attitude.

True and enduring happiness depends upon a close relationship with God our Father. Keep near to Him. Be happy, my dear readers, your Father in Heaven loves you and wants you to live a full, useful and beautiful life! "This is the day which the Lord hath made; we will rejoice and be glad in it." –Psalm 118:24.

Persistence of the Ant

"Just keep on keeping on and you will reach your goal with sure success!"

One of the greatest secrets of success, today, we will learn from a tiny ant.

There is no royal road over which we are carried to achieve anything noteworthy, one step at a time and each step in succession. That which steadily perseveres will endure.

The book of Proverbs says, "Go watch the ant, you who are not trying hard enough."

There was once a soldier who was forced to hide from his enemies in an abandoned cement silo. He had been on the run for days. Exhausted and weary, he almost gave up to hopelessness. As the solider looked down on the barren floor, there appeared a tiny ant. The insect was carrying a crumb of bread and was attempting to climb up the high, steep wall. The crumb kept falling, but the ant refused to give up. The man counted the ant's attempts to get the crumb up to a window to the outside.

The crumb fell seventy times to the ground. The soldier watched in incredible awe as each time the ant, again and again, patiently shouldered its burden and continued to try. The ant persevered. On the seventy-first time the insect reached the top. That tiny ant's persistence gave the man courage and hope to keep on trying. Two days later, freedom was his.

God sent His grace with a great example of encouragement in the form of a tiny ant. If you think nothing of importance is happening around you, then perhaps you are being too careless in your observation. Observe everything and everybody. And remember the saying, "Practice makes perfect."

Everyone has a reason for being here. If you have breath in your body you have a goal yet to still achieve. The best goal God recognizes is the goal you have that will help and uplift someone else. Persist to make the world a better place. You can do it. There is a way to make a difference. God blesses those who keep on trying. There must be something you can do for someone else. You can make your goal a certain number of smiles to give each day. If you give you will automatically receive. So give help, encouragement, and the joy of life to others.

If you want to write a book that you feel will help others, don't give up. If you want to paint a picture to give others insight to beauty, never quit. If you want to give your own family more joy, continue to persist.

Make something extraordinary out of your life. First your task will seem impossible. Then, it will be difficult. Finally with persistence it will get done!

If you only knew the love that God has for you and how beautiful you are in His sight, you would never be discouraged again. Pray to see yourself through His eyes and you will be amazed at how much more beautiful you become each day. God can reveal to you your true potential. You have so much talent and the ability to do anything! Just never give up! He made each person to accomplish something great. You were born with a great capacity for giving. All you need is a compassionate, caring heart committed to God and He will direct your path.

Even through adversity, keep on trying. God is with the person who refuses to quit. Eventually you will reach your destiny. So start today, ask God, "What can I do?" Get one of those bracelets with "W.W.J.D." on it and ask yourself daily, "What Would Jesus Do?" Somehow, you will begin to know what you are supposed to do to shed life, love and joy on the lives of others. You can do wonders. God placed a great ability for achievement in you. Just keep on keeping on and you will reach your goal with sure success!

Goose Sense

"We are here on earth to help one another."

The next time you happen to see geese flying along in a "V" formation, you may be interested to learn what science has discovered about why they fly in that unusual way.

As each bird flaps its wings, it creates an uplift for the bird immediately following. By flying in a "V" formation, the whole flock adds at least 71% greater flying range than if each bird flew on its own. The birds fly further when they fly together than if they flew alone. Each goose gets help from the previous one; they don't get as tired or use up as much of their energy.

Whenever a goose falls out of formation, it suddenly feels the drag and resistance of air in trying to go it alone and quickly gets back into formation to take advantage of the lifting power of the bird in front of him. When the lead goose gets tired, it rotates to the back of the formation and another goose takes the lead. The geese honk from behind to encourage those up in front to keep up their speed. And if a fellow goose gets sick or is wounded, two geese fall out of formation and follow the injured bird down to help, feed and protect it. They stay with it until it is able to fly on its own. Then they launch out to join another group.

We human beings should pay close attention to this valuable and beautiful lesson.

Albert Einstein once said, "The most important question a human being could answer is 'Is the universe a friendly place?'"

We are here on earth to help one another. The Bible says, "Let not everyone look after their own needs, but on the needs of another." There is strength built into your own character, as you stay close in touch with the needs of others, in your family or community. People who share a common direction and a sense of togetherness can get where they are going quicker and easier because they are traveling on the strength of one another.

Life is a journey. Going it alone is tough and hard. Unless we uphold each other and continually help one another we will never have the fulfillment of a joy filled life.

Be kinder than you have to be, more compassionate and more loving. When we give our best we increase the abundance of life in our children, our community, and in a larger sense, a rippling effect in the lives of strangers that we don't even see. The soul grows when it is giving and receiving love. "All my life I have noticed that when people care and do good for others, that that goodness gets returned over and over again," says a reader.

A symphony is a beautiful thing to watch and much like life should be. As the conductor begins, each instrument is in harmony one with the other. Then a violin begins to solo, the other instruments create a beautiful accompaniment of background music. Then the violin fades into the background and the flute starts to solo as the other instruments accompany it. The musicians do not vie for the lead and cause disharmony or walk off the stage because they are not in the lead for the moment. But they uphold each other to create beauty and form in the symphony. The musicians are much like the geese and much like our own family life, work life and social life should be.

Sticking close to each other in genuine love, upholding each other in prayer, protecting each other in kindness, feeding each other with encouragement… always reading the music, the word of God, and always watching HIM… the Conductor.

A Fabulous Work of Art

"In all the universe, there is no on else exactly like you."

Imagine yourself alone with your Creator, who pulled from His spirit an original work of art when He designed you. On His easel, He placed the canvas of your unique self. The paint used was the rainbow of His character and each bristle of the brush was alive with love. Using precise placement, expert skill and great compassion, God made each one of us to be a masterpiece. The spectacular beauty of the world to be as a background for us to live out the great drama of our lives.

Stop now, dear readers, and take a few moments to think about this awesome fact. You are a masterpiece. A fabulous work of art.

You are esteemed the most valuable object on earth. In all the universe, there is no on else exactly like you. You are truly one of a kind and are capable of great things.

You deserve the best. Start a file filled with pictures of dreams you may have discarded. A home filled with people to love, an exciting new business or a peaceful vacation. Tear out your pictures from books or magazines. Collect them to remind yourself that the future is filled with unlimited possibilities.

Nurture the childlike wonder within. Look at the world through the eyes of a child. Notice the purity of a snowflake, the purring of a kitten or the laughter of children in their games. Youngsters appreciate the simple things; a walk in the park, building a snowman or a bike ride around the neighborhood.

Imagine now, viewing your life when you're 90 years old. What do you wish you had done differently? Organize your priorities with 90 year old hindsight. Everyone can start again and anew no matter what age. It is only a thought away.

Think positive. Shed layers of self-doubt and you'll be pounds lighter! You and only you determine what thoughts, ideas and actions control you. You can move a mountain if you choose to. With God all things are possible.

Reflect inwardly. Pay attention to your inner voice. Choose wisely the kinds of places, people and situations you spend your precious time on. Utilize your energy only doing the things that will make you happy and help you grow as a person.

Speak aloud positive affirmations each day. Positive words can turn dreams into realities.

Consider paintings by Rembrandt, Monet or Hoffman. They have great value because they were created by masters and each piece a priceless work of art. Are you not of more value than these? You were made a masterpiece. Be thankful for the unique individual that you are. God's magnificent portrait just waiting to be unveiled.

God's Timing for Your Life is Ever Perfect

"God will give you all that you need and desire, but the time is not in your hands, the time is in His hands."

On God's clock there are no hands, minutes, hours or seconds. Just a beating of a heart, ticking away, in perfect love. Like clockwork, God's timing is always exact and perfect. Remember who is in control. God will give you all that you need and desire, but the time is not in your hands, the time is in His hands.

Some of us live, breath and race by the clock. Our watches set five minutes ahead, our car clocks, desk clocks, and our alarms ring constantly. In good times, I want the clock to stand still, right here and now, at this very moment. But, Father-time waits for no one. Time goes on and on and I believe will only get better and better as we get closer to His heart.

- Don't waste time. Time is your most precious commodity. Never waste it. Life is too short. Do as much as you can every day.
- Don't be impatient. With our allotted time here on earth we must practice patience. Wait on God to bring to pass all that He has promised. As you wait, rest in faith for what you can not see. At just the perfect time, He will provide everything that is good to bless your life.

- Utilize time. As you are waiting in traffic, at a line in the grocery store or at a doctors appointment, utilize that time to think about people who make you happy. Think on the good things in your life, your home, your pets and the beauty of nature. Whisper a prayer of thanks.
- Take time for the one you love. It's important to have people to love. Who knows what wondrous ways love can be awakened. Only God knows. You may meet someone by chance one day and that one moment can decide your destiny. And as my grandmother always said, "When the right one comes along, you'll know it." It takes only a minute to write a cute love note, attach it to the bathroom mirror with tape or to send a card to your spouse at work. Let your loved one know they are thought of often.
- Make time for God. Trust and love Him. Resolve to pray with greater originality and intimacy. God will alter time and make great things happen for you in your life as you make time for Him. God is good and life is wonderful. Open your heart to God and everything will be beautiful.
- Be sensitive to God's perfect timing. Many a time, I've called my friend to hear her exclaim with joy, "I can't believe you just called me! I was just thinking of you," she says. God's perfect timing again.

The sun rises to begin a fresh, new day. The sun sets at the cool of the evening. The warmth and illuminating rays of the summertime vanish into the bitter cold of the winter. The trees change, the leaves fall. Under the ice and snow, hidden to our sight, the life in the roots of the trees begins to rise again. God's timing is perfect. We too shall rise again after each bitter, cold experience we encounter because our lives and our time are in God's hands.

Unique Talents Make All of Us Truly Special

"It is each one of our purposes in life to offer the wonderful gifts we posses to the world."

Each one of us has been blessed with a unique gift to bring to this world. Equipped with our own personality, talents, and ambitions we all have something special that no one else can duplicate. As a human being, living in the twentieth century, you have a greater potential than anyone else who has ever lived before. A person holds the key to every situation and is made or unmade by his or her own self. You are the maker of your character, the molder of your life and the builder of your destiny. It is each one of our purposes in life to offer the wonderful gifts we posses to the world. Because of your own exceptional skills many others could benefit. Utilize your special talents to the fullest and make your life extraordinary!

Believe in yourself. Every person has different desires, aspirations and objectives. Choose to pursue whatever vision you have of yourself. Preserve your own identity. Only you know where the talents lie and what you enjoy doing. The greatest resource in the world is under our hats and stands in our shoes. It is our duty and responsibility to develop these assets.

Have a clear picture of what you wish to accomplish. Strong lives are motivated by dynamic purposes. The most successful individuals are but the reflection of an inner fire. Have a strong faith in your rare talents and find the courage to persevere even through adversity. Persistent effort often spells the difference between success and failure.

Be enthusiastic about what you are accomplishing. People who radiate enthusiasm are excited about the things they are doing and communicate the excitement to others. On one of my interviews, while promoting my concept of this column to an editor, I was told I had infectious energy. I was happy, elated and very enthusiastic about my innovative idea. My energy and excitement came out and affected those around me in a positive way.

Be strong and ask directly for what you want. Believe in the impossible and it can become possible. Do the things you imagine with your life. Don't be afraid of going after your goals with full force. One who cherishes a beautiful vision will one day realize it. Dreamers are the saviors of the world. Where would we be today without Christopher Columbus, Orville and Wilber Wright or Alexander Graham Bell? These individuals had a vision, worked hard and used their remarkable capabilities and succeeded.

Stay focused on your goals. Keep your mind fixed on achieving your every dream. Be firm in your convictions. Try and try again when a situation does not work out. Don't give up – work harder! There are seasons in all our lives that we experience a period of sorrow, difficulty and pain. But who knows what goodness lies ahead. Even the desert blooms after a storm. There is a purpose for everything that happens. Even during our darkest times, keep the hope and the faith that your misfortune will pass. There is always a seed of good in every bad situation. For whenever God shuts one door, somewhere He opens a window.

Make the most of the valuable qualities you have been blessed with. You are an exceptional and worthwhile human being. With all the attributes you posses, you have the power to do miraculous things with your life.

That's Tenacious with a Capital "T"

"I truly believe with patience, hard work and determination, your dreams can come true."

"Catherine, you are the most tenacious person I know," a general manager of a local television station said to me during a telephone conversation. Tenacious... I pondered over that word the entire day. Tenacious. When I arrived home that evening, I looked up tenacious in the dictionary. According to the American Heritage Dictionary, the word tenacious is defined as 1.Persistant 2.Cohesive or adhesive 3.Tending to retain: retentive. You know...like "crazy glue."

I always considered myself persevering. My philosophy in life is that if you want something badly enough, you can achieve it. I truly believe with patience, hard work and determination, your dreams can come true.

It may take many years. Is achieving your dream worth it? You may have to overcome amazing setbacks. There can be countless struggles, sacrifices and pain. But, if you have the tenacity, strong will and faith you will achieve your highest dreams.

The best prizes of life are not always given in the beginning of your journey. They are usually near the end. You never can tell how close you are toward your goal. When it seems so far away, take another step. It actually may be developing right around the corner.

Begin every day seeing yourself climbing to and arriving at the top of your mountain. The trials and undertakings of getting there can be very rewarding. The Bible says, "By sorrow the heart is made better." So, whether you feel it now or not, you are being made better day by day.

Follow up on every opportunity, each thought and all beneficial ideas that come into your mind. If you can't tackle your goal head on, attack it from another direction. When faced with a closed door, try other entries. If that approach doesn't work, keep trying until you find one that does.

Be content and pat yourself on the back for what you have accomplished already. Realize just how fortunate you are, having been blessed with the skills that are yours alone. If you are happy with yourself as a person, then when you get to your destination you will be ecstatic!

"I called on a prominent company for eight years to try to acquire their business," says the CEO of a major corporation. "After phoning 32 times in the eight year period, I finally got them," he points out enthusiastically. "This year, because of their business, we'll do well over one hundred million dollars."

I cannot predict the future, though this much I do know. If you have a burning desire to succeed and your ambitions are morally correct, and you pursue that objective with honesty, your plans will transpire.

The final decisions of your future are up to you. You can be anything that you want to be and do all that you dream of doing. But, be forewarned; don't dream without action.

I am building my castle one brick at a time. For I know that small attempts persistently will complete any task. So, yes I agree wholeheartedly, I am quite tenacious and proud of it!

Mother's Day

"If I could only go back in time and know then what I know now."

I dedicate this column to my mother and to beloved mothers everywhere. Mother's Day is a time of reflection and thanksgiving.

My heart stirs, as I search my mind to remember… It seems hard to believe that ten years has come and gone since my mother passed away. I recall her saying to me, "If I could only go back in time and know then what I know now." I try to recollect bits and pieces of her wisdom. But, if I only knew then what I know now… How I long today for my mother's gentle touch, keen observations and loving advice. It never occurred to me, even once, that she would be gone in the blink of an eye. If that insight was revealed to me, I would have savored every minute I had with her. I would have asked her a thousand questions and we would have shared so much more.

Mother's are the source from which we derive the guiding principles of life. It's been said, "The hand that rocks the cradle rules the world." George Washington wrote, "All I am, I owe to my mother. I attribute all my success in life to the moral, intellectual and physical education I received from her." A mother's heart is the classroom of a child. That love endures beyond time or death. My mother taught me to be kind. "Be nice and love everyone," she would say. I learned what it means to love unconditionally and to give up everything for your family. When you have a child, you only want what makes them happy, you forget yourself.

My mother's truth and insight still rings in my ear and the sweetness of the tone in her voice guides me onward. But, God has also sent me substitute mothers. "Angels," as I call them, who have helped me along the way and who give me strength and comfort. If you haven't been blessed with a wonderful mother, ask God to lead you to someone who has a real mother's heart. He has someone out there for you.

My mother and I had an unspoken trust. On Mother's Day, years ago, I placed a small box of chocolates with an "I love you" note attached, under my mother's pillow. She loved it and thus it became a ritual, not just on Mother's Day, but at other times too. We'd pass under-the-pillow notes and gifts from my pillow to hers. As a little girl, I recall asking mom not to show the notes to anyone… they were just for her and they'd be our little secret. So, she never spoke of our under-the-pillow messages.

Not a day goes by that I do not think about my precious mother. Writing this for you, dear readers, makes me tremble with a longing to hug her and tell her that I love her. Through my tears, I think it's important for you, my friends, to learn from my experience. So right now, today, while you still can, write those notes of appreciation, say those words of love and thankfulness and give your mother an extra long hug!

The day after my mother passed away, under her mattress, I found the little bundle of notes, cards and letters I gave to her, through the years, tied with a faded pink ribbon. Gently, I held the notes to my heart and whispered a prayer that has clung to me all my life. The greatest compliment I could say, "Lord, please, in all her good and kind ways, make me like my mother."

A Family's Love

"Love begins at home, so generate harmony, give out hugs, kind words, and positive praise."

As a young girl in the 1930's, my mother grew up in a closely knit neighborhood in New Haven. It was during the depression era when finances were almost non-existent. I remember her telling me stories about how things were in her family. My Grandfather, a good man as she described him, adored his wife and six daughters. They all lived in a small apartment and my grandfather worked two jobs to support his family. My grandmother, "Naunie" helped everybody; she never thought of herself, only of others. Whatever someone needed, she did it – cooking, baking, baby-sitting, or cleaning. We could never forget her.

"Everyone knew everyone," recalls an aunt. "Neighbors, relatives, and friends were all very close. We helped one another and shared what we had."

My mother's family never owned a house or a car. Their material possessions were few, but their home was filled with laughter, love, and happiness. They never lacked in the most important gift of all, the cherished treasure of unconditional love.

Of all the special blessings from God, love is the greatest. As the Bible says, "Now abides faith, hope, and love…but the greatest of these is love." –1 Corinthians 13:13.

The capacity and need to love and to be loved is within each of us. God set the example; He did all things in love. He gave us each other so we would not walk alone. No great material possession can replace the gift of your own unique and spontaneous love expressed to others.

Love begins at home, so generate harmony, give out hugs, kind words, and positive praise. Have fun together. "Laughter is one of the best gifts," says a reader. "When you laugh you feel good and make others happy." A home with a shared and kind sense of humor will bring joyful and sweet memories.

Give the gift of yourself. Be liberal with your attention and affection to those you love. Promote family gatherings. Have one family meal together each day. Mealtime can give you a chance to talk to one another and to enjoy the time spent with your precious family. Have open communication. Just being there to talk and listen to a family member or friend who needs support can help to solve problems, remove stress, and comfort them so that they overcome their obstacles. Communication is the source of life.

Be caring and encouraging to those you love. Believe in and expect the best of them. Have an unspoken trust. Loyalty will bind you together. The joy you experience with your family will spill out over to your neighbors and pass kindness along in your community. "Society needs to encourage people to do the right things," says a reader. "Give kindness and support to others and you will be rewarded for doing good." Open your hands and your heart to others. When you give the gifts that money cannot buy, your heart will be filled with heaven's peace. We can each create a new earth filled with serenity and contentment. Share your life with those around you.

These are some of the values that my grandparents instilled in my mother. And I hope to pass them on to my own children one day. So beyond the material presents, decorations, and celebrations this month, let's reflect on the closeness, the sharing and the love of our dear family and trusted friends. This constitutes the unconditional loving, caring, and respect that is to be treasured for all generations.

When I think on these things, I can feel the warmth of my mother, my grandmother and grandfather, as their hands are joined together, smiling down on me from Heaven…as their legacy of heart continues…

Sow and Reap

"Positively influencing another person's life will make your own life brighter as a result."

"Judge each day not by the harvest you reap, but by the seeds that you plant." –Robert Louis Stevenson.

What you deliver with one hand, you will gather with two. It is the natural law of the universe, the alpha (beginning) and omega (end). The encouragement, help and happiness that you share with others will come back full circle to you. Everything that goes around, comes around.

Positively influencing another person's life will make your own life brighter as a result. Giving to others without a thought of payment or reward can help to make the world a better place for yourself, your family and your fellow human beings. One person can make a difference.

We will reap exactly what we sow, good or evil. Every good deed will beget good results and bad will bring bad results. Know that, "Whatever sows sparingly will also reap sparingly and whoever sows generously will also reap generously." –Corinthians 7:6. God is able to make all things come to you, so in all that you do, be overflowing in goodness to His children, as an expression of thanks for the abundance of blessings and talents that He has bestowed upon you.

- Shower unconditional love onto others. Love was not put into your heart to stay, but it was made to be given away! Bring a ray of sunshine to others. Bake cookies for a classroom treat, share a book with a friend that means much to you or have tea with a person who has no company.
- Teach children to perform good deeds. On a snowy day, encourage them to shovel a neighbors driveway, to care for a friend's pet while they are on vacation or to donate a part of their allowance to a needy charity. Discuss with the child the importance of giving and doing for others.
- Get involved in the community. "I go to area convalescent homes and play the accordion," says an area musician. "The elderly enjoy singing along and the music cheers them up," he says. "It makes me feel so good to see them happy."
- Your deeds don't have to be elaborate. Grocery shop for someone who is sick. Do laundry, go to the bank or pay bills for an older person. Offer to drive a neighbor to the doctor if they are having medical tests taken.
- It makes a person feel good to help those in need. A recent study revealed that people who did volunteer work at least once a week outlived those who did none. That implies that doing something for another is a powerful contributor to health and a long life.

The memory of your good deed can be eternal. When we leave this world, let our legacy be that we left it a better place than when we found it. "The greatest use of life is to spend it for something that will outlast it," wrote William James.

If each one of us did just one good deed a day, imagine what kind of world we would live in. So, let me leave you today, dear readers, with a passage from Galatians 6:9. "And let us not be weary in well doing; for in due season, we shall reap, if we faint not."

You are a wonderful individual, share your unique self with the world so that others can benefit and you will become a leader among all human beings. As this column comes to a close, I feel so happy. The joy I've shared with you has come back and filled my heart. See... it works!

Stay Calm and the Dark Times Will Pass

"Life is a circle of moods. Just as the tides advance and recede, our feelings can turn from happiness to melancholy, from bliss to sadness."

At times in all our lives, it is so difficult to persevere when all of the odds seems stacked up against us. When every day is an uphill climb. Where we feel sad, afraid and depressed.

Well, take heart, you are not alone in these feelings. For most of us, at some point in our lives experience these periods. Sometimes, we want to give up, but together we will overcome our negative emotions and persevere. Let's persist knowing that it is quite natural for our emotions to be up and sometimes down.

Life is a circle of moods. Just as the tides advance and recede, our feelings can turn from happiness to melancholy; from bliss to sadness. Human beings are a part of nature. Therefor, like the tides, it is expected that our emotions will, from time to time, rise and fall.

We can control our emotions by controlling the influences in our lives. It is how we react to these influences that determines the course of the future. When you get discouraged and you feel as though you want to quit, there is one thing that you can do. Surround yourself with positive friendship. We all know many people whom we can call friends, but if we have two we can call on when everything goes wrong and they listen, we're rich indeed.

If a predicament looks hopeless, keep in mind that there is no situation so completely dark that something constructive cannot be done about it. Maintain a positive outlook and a sense of hope. When faced with a minus, ask yourself what you can do to make it a plus. Reject hopelessness, substitute confidence. Use persistent effort and you can lift yourself out of your blue mood.

Try not to act emotionally when a problem arises. Think about the situation and use your rational thought process to solve the issue, eliminate it or develop an idea pattern that will enable you to live with the situation. "And this too shall pass," is a favorite saying of mine when things are not going as they should.

Never let your emotions overwhelm you. Think of something kind you can do for someone else. Helping others can elevate your mood until the storm passes.

Like beautiful flowers, today's full bloom of joy can fade and wither into a temporary sorrow. Yet, always remember that the wilting flower carries the seed of tomorrow's magnificent and vibrant full bloom. Therefor, so does this day's sadness bear the seed of tomorrow's exhilaration and happiness. God bless you and keep you.

Destiny

"There is nothing as beautiful as meeting the one mate that was destined just for you."

God loves the world so much that He shows His love in all nature. And among the shining, brilliant stars, the deep, blue ocean and rainbows in a multitude of glorious hues, there is no example as precious as the genuine love, truly felt between a man and a woman. There is nothing as beautiful as meeting the one mate that was destined just for you. When your eyes meet, deep in your heart, you know that this is the person that God made to be the other half of you.

Your search for your mate may be long and weary and the road obstructed with tears and pain. But when romance does finally bloom, a new life begins for both of you. Life before you met seems like a deep sleep.

In days past, marriages were arranged. Now, we have the power to choose. Select your life's partner wisely. This one decision can contribute a great deal to your happiness or unhappiness. Take inventory of the person's heart and it will reveal what's inside. Observe their character, meet their friends, their family. What kind of pictures do they have hanging on their wall? What is their choice of music, hobbies and books? Look around, be aware and listen to the words that they speak... Your life is so valuable. Be careful and use wisdom. "Guard your heart, for it is the wellspring of life." –Proverbs 4:23.

You may meet someone by chance one day and that moment could decide your destiny. "My wife and I got engaged after two weeks," recalls a local man. "When I met her, I just knew she was the woman I would marry," he says. "It has been 20 years and our relationship is better than ever!" True love will grow as the years go by. Through the lengthening shadows of life, love sends it's golden rays of beauty and strength into your union.

Share common interests, goals and values. Have fun together. Enjoyable experiences, laughter and new activities can keep your relationship fresh and exciting. Build friendship skills. In successful marriages, partners are best friends. Go on weekend excursions, have candlelight dinners and spend time alone, talking in front of the fireplace. Share personal thoughts and be supportive of your loved one's dreams and goals. Know that your spouse can't always read your mind, so compliment them. Acknowledge the great dinner that they cooked, say that you enjoy their company and you appreciate their hard work. The more expressive you are, the more your love will grow.

It is important to give each other attention and affection. A tender touch can mean so much. Praise your partner's character, their redeeming qualities and traits. This is the person that you promised to love, honor and keep. Send a loving card, give a small gift or write a poem. The littlest gesture, done in love, can make the biggest impact.

Let petty differences slide by. Handle conflicts by trying to see the other persons point of view. Think before you speak. Be understanding and compromise; focus on what you can do to make the situation better. Do not name call or belittle each other. Refuse any negative feelings. "A soft answer turneth away wrath; but grievous words stir up anger." –Proverbs 15:1.

Pray together and share spiritual experiences. Read passages from the Bible, take on a project at church and help a family in need. A close communion with God can give you the strength to face any challenges that lie ahead.

Just as the dawn comes out of the darkness of the night, love can materialize out of your dreams and into your life. Love, like a bouquet of beautiful roses, is sent from heaven, delivered by the angelic hands of angels and is our greatest blessing from God.

Shining Gem of Hope

"What a formula: perseverance coupled with hope equals success."

She wore it around her neck and never took it off. When she was afraid, she'd touch it and a calm would settle over her. If she was lonely, she would gaze at it and smile and when she was sad, because of it, she would become happy.

Years ago, her dear grandfather gave her the heart shaped sealed locket. And this precious piece of jewelry, he told her, contained a valuable, rare diamond. "If there's ever a time you are in need," said the grandfather to the young girl, "you can break open the locket, sell the diamond and make it through the difficulty."

Days, months, and years passed as the young girl grew into womanhood. She struggled though much adversity, poverty and need. There were moments that she thought she couldn't go on any longer. But just the comforting thought of the diamond locket that her grandfather gave to her, that she wore safely around her neck, gave her courage.

With much prayer, perseverance and determination, the dreams of this young woman were one by one being fulfilled. No longer in financial need she showed the locket to a jeweler friend and told him about her grandfather's special gift. Her friend asked if he could appraise the diamond in the locket. As the jeweler studied the stone he said stunned, "Why, this is a perfect diamond… If you sold it, it would have saved you much struggle and stress." The woman, with tear filled eyes said, "I could never sell it. It is a symbol of something much more valuable… the precious treasure of my grandfathers love."

Love is the priceless gem her grandfather gave her. It was a gift of hope, of encouragement and the confidence to know that everything could be all right. For love is a treasure beyond the monetary value of a perfect gem.

Hope is joyful expectation. It knows with certainty that all things do work together for good.

Live with hope in your heart, your mind and your actions and you will have discovered one of life's most powerful secrets of happiness.

Hope can help you to never give up. Have faith and patience and your dreams of achieving real happiness in life will come true. Obstacles don't have to stop you. If you run into a wall, climb up over it, walk around it or tunnel through it. You'll make it! What a formula: perseverance coupled with hope equals success.

Picture in your mind achieving the goal you desire and that thought will transform your life into that victorious individual. We become what our thoughts and hearts are fixed upon.

When you choose the highest, you pay a price. Be willing to do so. Stand for what's right and true. Let criticism bounce off you, be willing to stand alone with God at your side.

Character is built through overcoming adversity. The loss of pride is a small price to pay to keep your honor. I would rather stand alone for what is right, then to be encircled in a crowd of compromisers. There comes a time when we reap what we have sown, chaos or peace. Robert Frost said it perfectly when he wrote, "Two roads diverged in a wood, and I… I took the one less traveled by, and that has made all the difference."

You must put the right thoughts continually into your mind and stand for them. Guard carefully what you read, watch and listen to. Surround yourself with noble things, the precious positives of the Word of God.

Think, talk and act hopeful about everything. As you do, hopefulness takes over and produces the fact.

Hope is so close; all we have to do is ask, believe and expect.

By living for Him you become God's perfect gem… a sparkling jewel in His crown.

A Blessed Event

"A new baby is like the beginning of all things, wonder, hope and a dream of possibilities."

My earliest recollection of my mother was calling her name out in the middle of the night so she could console and enfold me safe in her arms and rock me back to sleep with her gentle touch of reassurance. As the years unfolded, she became my playmate, playing hopscotch with me, adjusting my training wheels and braiding my dolls hair. Mother would gladly give up new shoes for her feet to let her children have a new pair.

The thought of my mom is still precious and fresh in my mind. I think of the picture of her when she was eight months pregnant with me. "I gained 40 pounds with you and craved oranges," she would say. How priceless those memories are, even years and years after she went to heaven. A good mother gives so much of herself, becoming a counselor, teacher, friend, disciplinarian, comforter… a good mother is so many things.

Never miss an opportunity to show your children what it means to be a loving person. Steadfast love is what sustains a child through times of turmoil. A parent's example, words and attitude set the stage for a child's future development. Provide an atmosphere of emotional comfort, a place of peace and security in your home, letting their friends be welcome there. The ornament of a house is the warmth of hospitality and love to all who dwell in it.

Mothers also need to take special care of themselves on a regular basis in order to keep up with the demands placed on their time. A father's involvement is equally important to the well being of the family, a strong character, confident and full of faith.

"Husbands: love your wife as your own self." –Ephesians 5:28-30. Give your wife special attention, reassurance and understanding. Value her opinion and listen to her. Let both of you teach your children about God. Awaken them to higher things.

Show them a respectful nature, compassion, honesty, generosity and traditional values.

A new baby is like the beginning of all things, wonder, hope and a dream of possibilities.

William Branham once said, "An angel is always around a woman who is expecting a baby." I believe the angels leave, with the new mother and child, their influence and bring out the best that God intended a mother to be. Whenever I have held a little newborn and seen it look over my shoulder and smile at something behind and above me, I'm sure that the baby still sees the angels. God is so gracious to blend this dimension with the heavenly for the first few weeks of this new life.

I once read a quote from an eighteenth century writer who said, "God sends children for another purpose than merely to keep up the race, but… to enlarge our hearts and to make us unselfish and full of kindly sympathies and affections; to give our souls higher aims and to bring round our firesides bright faces, happy smiles and loving, tender hearts."

Every true mother's heart continually gives love to others long after their children are grown and gone from the home. For they know that everyone has a great need for loving attention. So even though you may not have children of your own, there is in many an adult, a lonely child crying out for love and understanding, so give freely and rejoice in the opportunity to do so. We all need to be loved and cared for.

Because of the example of motherhood given to me, I have longed for many a year for the chance to one day be a mother, to hold and mold a little life to be the light God meant it to be in this world.

And wonders of wonders, dear readers, God has blessed me and my husband with the expectation of our first child in the coming fall. One of the many songs I will sing to it will be, "This little light of mine, I'm going to let it shine, let it shine, let it shine."

I am so happy to be able to share this blessed news with you.

Kindness Counts

"I believe that niceness and what's inside counts."

"I totally agree with what you are saying in your article," wrote, a 12-year-old reader. "I believe that niceness and what's inside counts. I have a neurological disorder called Tourette Syndrome that causes me to constantly tic," wrote the student. "All of my friends, family and teachers at school are understanding, kind and loving to me. I do many kind things and help people, little things, here and there," she wrote. "I get this good feeling inside when I do something kind for someone. Some people think I'm almost 'too nice'... but I don't think there's such a thing."

There is a shining quality of goodness that radiates from individuals who know how important it is to be kind. Such people, strangers, family members or friends alike, can change the quality of life for others... just by their mere presence. "Happy are those who are kind." –Proverbs 14:21.

The word kind comes from the Old English cynd for kin or family. It is first within the home that we learn to respect and care for others. Share the gift of your time, attention and affection with those you love. Promote family togetherness. Sometimes, it is easy to take those closest to you for granted, so each day be sure to give a compliment, a warm embrace and a word of appreciation to your loved ones. These are precious gifts that nothing else can replace.

Each relationship we encounter is one of giving and taking. The more you give away, the more you will receive. Anything of worth in life only multiplies when it is shared or given. Consider investing in people as much as you would the stocks, bonds or the bank. The stock exchange and the banks may fail you long before the people who have helped you will.

Develop a thoughtful attitude. Put yourself in another person's place and respect his point of view. The Indians have a saying, "Walk in his moccasins." Be sensitive to another's feelings. Tactless comments, foolish questions or jokes about another's looks, background or beliefs can be hurtful. While kindness can change the life of another in a positive way. Silently pray for someone. Prayer is always positive. Ask God to bless people with the good things in life and your own life will be bliss!

Many words, benevolence, goodheartedness and consideration express the moment when a good thought transforms into a good deed or when a generous gesture touches the life of another. Being kind matters. We all have difficulties to face and challenges from day to day, and there is a common quality among those who have suffered. They now have a life filled with compassion. Compassion is the ability to understand with tenderheartedness and kindness. It is the longing to help others go through difficult times because you yourself have experienced these trials. "Comfort others with the comfort I have given you," the Bible says.

My 12-year-old reader has managed to grasp kindness – one of the true meanings of life – at such an early age. Today, whoever you encounter, encourage and comfort them. It may be a compliment, just a smile or a simple hello. Begin the process of circulating joy and miraculous effects will follow. God Bless you, my dear readers... You mean so much to me.

Your Word Can Create a Better Life

"The words you express are the windows to your heart."

Before I begin each column, I pray that the Lord will give me the right "words" to write and touch the heart of each one of you and give you the secrets I've found of success for living. Today, I am sharing one of my greatest secrets... Say only the things that you want to happen in your life. The words you express are the windows to your heart. "For out of the abundance of the heart the mouth speaks." –Matthew 12:34.

What you "say" says a lot about you. We reveal so much, just in every day conversation.

Words are our primary source of communication. They are powerful tools that should be used with extreme wisdom. Words that are encouraging and spoken in love can bring about a new awakening into the lives of others. When you speak with love, you plant strength, hope and the power of transformation into another persons heart.

God wants us to communicate for the good of all. Phrases like, "Good work" "Can I help?" "I'm proud of you" "It is going to be all right," and "I love you," can be music to the recipient's ears! Your words can comfort, help and inspire and can be like a healing oil poured into the body of another. Each time we speak positive thoughts, we deliver our own souls into the realm where all things are possible. Hopeful words are like a pebble that is dropped into a lake, circles upon circles of sound waves ever expanding the joys of life.

You create the atmosphere around you. The words that come from your lips can bring happiness to yourself and those in which you come into contact with. Speak words of kindness, consideration and encouragement. Soon, you will begin to act and think on that basis. Grab for those words that are good, lovely and productive. If a negative word comes into your mind, immediately cancel it out and replace it with a positive thought and phrase.

Consider the words that are used when talking to our precious children. Criticism, put-downs, even when delivered "in fun" can hurt feeling and stunt the growth of a healthy self-image. Words spoken in anger can deeply wound and have lasting effects. "Let no corrupt communication proceed out of your mouth, but that which is good to the use of edifying, that it may minister grace unto the hearers." –Ephesians 4:29. If your words do not build-up or encourage another it is better to say nothing at all.

Taking the time to wish others a "good day," spending a moment praising a child or encouraging a friend, not only displays to others that we care, but also shows them how to care too. The cheer we spread will bring forth fruit in due season. "Love grows as it is given away," wrote a reader via e-mail, from Yale University's Divinity School, "…unlike many things we give away, love just multiplies and there is always more to give as well as to receive…so long as our hearts remain open." So, "say it" with love.

Take time to really care, give honest answers from the heart.

"A word aptly spoken is like apples of gold in settings of silver." –Proverbs 25.

Affirm only the best for yourself. You are worthy to receive all that you ask. You can have what you say and your body will obey your words. You can talk yourself into anything. So, be transformed by the renewing of your mind and by the words of your own mouth. At this moment say, "I am happier than I have ever been in my life because……" Fill in the space. Say exactly what you want then go and do it! Start now to create beautiful friendships, ladders to success and a joy filled life.

Faith in Yourself and God Gets You Through

"We are all challenged from time to time. Sometimes we feel like quitting. But, together we will continue to persevere."

"If you had faith as a grain of mustard seed you could say to this sycamine tree be rooted up and be planted in the sea and it would obey you." –Luke 17:15.

A mustard seed is very tiny and grows into a spinach-like bush. "Although the seed can be hybridized with other forms of mustards, it will not cross with any other kinds of plants," said an employee from the Connecticut Agricultural Experiment Station. This minute seed will not accept anything else but its own pure and destined purpose.

Our faith should be like the mustard seed, refusing to be connected with any negative feelings, doubts or fears.

We are all challenged from time to time. Sometimes we feel like quitting. But, together we will continue to persevere. The every day hurdles are mere obstacles to be overcome on the way to our goals. Let's all observe these guidelines to revive our faith.

❦ Recall past victories. Think back when your faith was tested and triumphed over defeat. "It was very difficult to find a university position when I came here from Canada," stated a local doctor. "I could have wallpapered my walls with the rejection letters that I received when applying to schools." Don't ever give up on a dream. Keep on trying and you will achieve it.

- ❦ Reaffirm what you want. Put your life into perspective. Organize your thoughts and ideas. Write down your aspirations and make a detailed list of what you want. Set goals for every month and as soon as you reach them set new ones. Aim higher! We are all on this earth for a short period and should make the most with the allotted time that we have.
- ❦ Reject discouragement. Do not allow hurtful words from others to rob you of your faith and belief in yourself. Learn to resist discouraging influences. Discouragement from individuals can be your greatest enemy. "Years ago, I wanted to go to the Culinary Institute to be a chef. My parents told me that I could not make it and I should be content as a printer," said a local man. "I am sorry that I listened to them and instead I wish I followed my own dreams. But, who knows maybe someday I will go to school and be the chef I wanted to be," the printer chuckled.
- ❦ Respond with positive confessions of faith. Words are powerful. Say exactly what you desire and ultimately it will happen. Don't be shy; go after what you want. Eliminate uncertainty from your mind and move forward towards your goals with an incontestable faith that your plans will succeed.
- ❦ Rely on God; He will take care of your needs. When our faith is challenged, count on the Lord's strength and wisdom. Trust that He will guide you to the life that He wants you to live and where you will best serve His purpose.
- ❦ Recognize the victory. Have a picture in your mind of what you want. Visualize your dreams coming true. Is it a home that you want? Start decorating it in your mind. A career change? Make plans on how you will begin your journey towards attaining it.

Believe in yourself, continue to pray and keep the faith. Miracles happen every day!

Vow to Put Worry Out of Your Mind

"God can do much more through your faith than He can through your worry."

"Therefor I tell you, do not worry about your life, what you will eat or drink; or about your body, what you will wear. Is life more important than food and the body more important than clothes. Look at the birds in the air; They do not sow or reap or store away in barns and yet your heavenly Father feeds them. Are you not much more valuable than they? Who of you by worrying can add a single hour to your life?" –Matthew 6:25-27.

Take a moment to think about this, dear readers. God can do much more through your faith than He can through your worry.

Most of the time, what we worry about never comes to pass. The average person will find that almost 90% of one's fears never happen. Do not worry about the future. Focus on the present. When we live for the present, the future takes care of itself.

This is a fresh, new day. Leave worry and anxiety behind. Enjoy the happiness that only this day can bring. God's mercy is fresh each morning.

Be too busy to worry. Try new and exciting things. Make life an adventure. Find joy and spread it generously. Cast away fears with faith in the right choices. Roosevelt said, "We have nothing to fear but fear itself." You have the ability to accomplish what has seemed to others to be impossible. Faith in He who is greater than yourself banishes fear. Believe that your life, your work and your contributions are important to both God and your fellow human beings.

Stay calm. If something happens to upset or worry you just be calm. Give your emotions a day to settle. Then, rationally discuss your concerns with the persons involved. Getting the problem off of your chest helps to put things into perspective. Don't hold emotions inside. Many health disorders have their beginnings in a negative emotional state such as anger, stress, frustration or worry. To avoid emotions building up, talk situations over with someone who loves you and whose opinion you respect. A call to a trusted friend can help you feel better. There are many support groups throughout the country that can help those in need. No one can understand your hurt like someone who has experienced it.

Shared laughter can lighten the load. Cultivate a sense of humor. Find the humor in every situation. Mentally ask yourself, "What's funny about this?" Anger, stress and worry will melt away with laughter.

Everyone feels apprehensive from time to time. Regardless of who you are, where you are or what you do, you are worth everything to God. He is watching over you and regards you highly. He has promised that all things work together for good to those who love Him. You may not see it right away, but later, down the road you will know it. So, do not worry.

The next time you visit the shoreline, take notice of the tiny birds far out in the ocean. No matter how high the waves or how rough the seas, you can see these small creatures with folded wings, quietly resting, perfectly secure, riding on top of the highest and roughest wave. The birds do not worry. They are not fearful. They know their Creator. You can ride the waves of life and overcome any obstacles because you are magnificent and of such great value to God our Father.

Kids of Today Can Give Hope for Tomorrow

"Make your child feel special. Reinforce their worth with loving and caring words and actions."

I was just a child with a little girls idea of what would be the most fun. "Oh, no," I cried, "It's a boy!" I was really upset, as my brother-in-law walked out of the hospital's delivery room to announce the birth of his new, five pound son. "But," I whined, "I wanted it to be a girl, so I could have someone to play with." Moments later, when I saw the miracle of my brand new nephew, I knew that male or female didn't matter. He was a precious new member of the family and I loved him immediately. All of my childish disappointments disappeared. Twenty years have passed and the family has grown with six more darling nephews and two sweet nieces. And guess who is the loving babysitter of them all.

The children of today are the country's future and the caretakers of tomorrow. They are tender, young creatures and need to be guided, nurtured and encouraged. I heard a quote recently that said, "A genius is someone who had a good mother." Parents need to make their children feel loved.

Pay attention to your children. Spend time talking and listening to your child's needs. On a daily basis, parents should ask their child what they did that day and get to know the friends that the child associates with. "Many kids seem to have too much free or unstructured time after school," says a Director of a Children and Adolescent Day Hospital. "Let kids have other outlets," she recommends, "fill their time with sports and hobbies that interest them."

Keep your children busy. Having creative outlets can help children feel good about themselves and their accomplishments. Parents, don't be afraid to set the limits for your children. They want you to validate that there are guidelines. Setting the limits to a child's emotions and activities can bring security, maturity and a well-balanced life.

Make your child feel special. Reinforce their worth with loving and caring words and actions. Read your child a bedtime story, create new family traditions, attend events that your child is a part of and plan special outings together.

The unconditional love of relatives and friends can give light and hope to teenagers and young adults as they begin to face this sometimes complicated world. Grandparents can enlighten the path of the little ones with stories of yesteryear. You are never too young or too old to encourage someone, to hand out a smile or speak a kind word. What we say to others can either shed light on their path or take it away. When it's a struggle to find the right words, a hug or touch of the hand can also express how deeply you care. Let the children of today know that they are worth a fortune and are wonderful, beautiful creations.

A Wonderful Sense of Humor

"Laughter is medicine for the bones"

Humor is one of God's marvelous gifts. Humor gives us smiles, laughter and fun. It reveals the roses and helps to hide the thorns. It softens the harshness of life for you and for others. Humor makes our heavy burdens light, smoothes the rough spots in our paths and eases the tension in our heavy workloads. A Chinese proverb tells us that, "Happiness never decreases by being shared." So share the gift of a wonderful and hearty sense of humor with someone else.

Studies show that laughter reduces pain, and increases alertness and energy. It can be a powerful antidote to stress. When you smile, your facial muscles press against nerves that release chemicals in the brain that give you a sense of well-being. Doctors find that it seems to promote the healing of the body. God's Word says, "Laughter is medicine for the bones," and "A merry heart doeth good like a medicine."

If you feel you have lost your sense of humor ask God for one and He will gladly give it to you. His Word says it is for your own good. So begin to look for that sense of humor to pop up in all aspects of your life. Forget the mistakes of the past, God loves you. Remember the old saying, "laugh and the world will laugh with you."

A reader wrote, "Way back in elementary school, my mom wrote in my autograph book a verse I will always recall, 'The world is like a mirror, reflecting what you do, and if you face it smiling it smiles right back at you.'"

I like the verse in the Bible that says, "The Lord loves an even balance."

Find time to relax and watch the squirrels at play and keep the enemy from blowing fears out of proportion. Humor helps to keep things in perspective and a sense of humor can help us smooth over disappointments and adversities. It's the delightful balm that can turn your difficulty into a source of strength. "You will have pain but your pain will turn to joy." –John 16:20.

People who look at the lighter side of life are less often depressed and bounce back quicker from sad events; they tend to have better health and may even live longer. They lift their mind above life's little irritations and keep their cool. Keep your emotions in balance, and do not to let petty things annoy or disturb you. Make the best of every situation and never lose your ability to laugh at yourself and at life. If a situation is troubling you share it with a trusted friend once and put it in God's hands. Try not to talk about it over and over again. If you don't keep rehashing the circumstances in your mind, eventually its effect on you will loose its power and fade away. Your joy will return quickly as you brighten up your day by doing something kind and unexpected for someone who is feeling down.

Maybe you can clip a cartoon from the newspaper and send it to a friend. Smile and nod a "hello" to everyone you see. Send a warm thank you note to a person who has enriched your life. Enjoy the companionship of loved ones and friends. Laughter can spark creativity, so inject humor into your business environment in memos or meetings. Bring good cheer wherever you go and find happiness in the simple things of life. Count your blessings and thank God for giving you another precious day.

Soon, you will be able to sing like the psalmist, "You have turned my mourning into dancing and clothed me with joy." –Psalm 30:11.

Have a happy heart, dear ones.

The Indian Chief

"What you will be next week is what you have said or done today."

An old Indian chief once said to a young preacher, "Ever since I have given my heart to God I find that within me there is a fight between the black dog and the white dog." Listening in amazement, the preacher asked, "Chief, which one wins?" The wise old chief remained silent for quite a few moments, then he gave a very profound answer… "The one that I feed the most."

Each and every day we pray for strength and wisdom to do our best. What you will be next week is what you have said or done today. The power that will be the strongest tomorrow is the one you have fed this day.

What do you and your family watch on television; what are the words to the music you are listening to? Does it promote violence and hate or peace and love? To be happy you must grasp with open arms all the loveliness of the world. God has shown you what He likes in His beautiful creation and has painted a masterpiece for you to see. The lovely dappled pattern on the road of sunlight filtering through the leaves. After a rainfall, witness the multitude of colors in the magnificent rainbow. Smile and say "hello" to a stranger and see their eyes light up and smile back. Every kind word and deed is feeding the white dog.

What thoughts do you play over and over again in your mind? It is universally known that what you think you will become.

We must strive for peace, joy and contentment – food for the right mental attitude. Our thoughts are the basic foundation of our character, our happiness, successes or failures. Thoughts produce feelings positive or negative and feelings control our action or inaction. A very simple children's story holds the proven key to every success. The little engine that said over and over and over again, "I think I can, I think I can, I think I can..." and guess what? He could. In order to think "we can" we have to feed positive images into our mind, actual pictures of every single step of our success. If you use your imagination to worry, change it to picture the successful outcome of every problem. If you use your memory to remember your hurts and failures, change it to remember the sweet and beautiful things of your life. Stop feeding the black dog and begin to feed the white dog with powerful truths. Stock the pantry of your heart with row upon row of life-giving food from: the Bible, the wisdom of philosophers and sages, inspirational poetry, music and art, even the advice of a trusted friend.

A definite time set aside at the beginning of each day to give thanks, ask for guidance and leadership to the open door of God's will is the key to ultimate victory. During your day, resolve to help someone in some small way, at least once in the morning and again in the afternoon. A deliberate act of courtesy and kindness, a short note sent to someone who has a need, a token of generosity or a few reassuring words will brighten their day. And good deeds will return in a miraculous way to create in you that Supreme Love that never fails, for these are God's acts and His ways.

At the end of the day, the last thing left in the subconscious feeds the soul all through the night. Let it be an act of putting into God's care any unsolved problem, for with the dawns light, will come the solution.

Philippians 4 encourages us to think, "Whatsoever things are true, whatsoever things are honest, whatsoever things are just, whatsoever things are pure, whatsoever things are lovely, whatsoever things are of good report – if there be any virtue (strength) or any praise (happiness) – you MUST think on these things."

That is a law written in the word of God. A law as positive and proven as the law of gravity. A law to bring you happiness and strength. So that when battles come you will be fortified and strengthened to always be the victor.

I Think I Can is a Mantra That Works

"If you believe you can, chances are you will."

Years ago, my nephew Steven was competing in the USS swim-meet championships at a local High School. He and the final five competitors stood on the staring block ready to begin the last phase of the competition. The starter's pistol sounded and the six swimmers expectantly dove into the crisp, clear water of the pool. My nephew's toughest competitor was swimming freestyle to his right and was ahead of the group. "When I saw that he was ahead," my nephew recalls, "I said to myself, 'you have nothing to lose, swim faster.'" Still my nephew stayed behind, but gained speed after the flip-turn. Undaunted, he said to himself again, "Come on, don't give up." Looking through fogged goggles, my nephew tried one last time to sprint his way past his opponent. With extra effort and confidence he thought, "I am going to win this race." Ten yards from the finish line Steven took off like a motor boat, plunged ahead of the competition, and won!

Your confidence of achievement at the beginning of any venture is all that is needed to finish the race and to dart ahead of the competition.

The word confidence comes from "confide," which means to trust. Having self-confidence is a matter of learning to trust yourself and your amazing abilities. Have confidence within yourself, then you can create that feeling in others.

- A lot of your self-confidence is formed in your adolescent years. A supportive family environment can make a boy or a girl feel good about themselves and can set the stage for positive self-confidence and achievement. "I tell my children that they can achieve anything that they want in life," says a father of four, "and to never say the word can't."
- Confident people focus on what they do well in life. Make a lengthy list of your best qualities and keep it in you wallet. Look at your list if you feel down and realize just how wonderful you are.
- Control any negative self-talk. The tongue is one of the hardest things to tame, but if you can control it you have mastered a great obstacle. Do not make any negative statements about yourself. This kind of talk is bad because if you tell yourself something over and over again, you begin to believe it. On the contrary, remind yourself continually that you are special and worthy of great things.
- Visualize yourself making progress toward your dreams. This can give you reason to feel good about yourself. It can also give you confidence needed to take the next step in realizing that goal. Any new venture can be scary at first, but you gain strength, courage and confidence by each experience in which you look fear in the face and continue onward.
- Forget guilt or regret. Force past failures out of your mind once you have learned from your error. We all make mistakes; don't think, what if... think of what's next. Put what is past into perspective and look at mistakes as your stepping stones.

- ❦ Use positive posture. Whether you are sitting, standing or walking, keep your chest out, shoulders squared, chin up and head held high. Walk with a snappy step, moving confidently toward your goal.
- ❦ Believe in yourself. Be strong in your convictions. Believing in yourself will give you the confidence needed to make things happen. If you believe you can, chances are you will.

I always told my nephew that he could be whatever he wanted to be and to do all that he dreamed of doing. I think a little of me must have rubbed off on him. And now, my dear readers, I am going to help you have the confidence in yourself, to persevere and to swim to victory.

Diet and Exercise for Good Health

"Lovingly care for this God given temple"

"If you have your health you have just about everything." A phrase we have all heard that is so true.

One of the best gifts we can give ourselves is to nurture and take care of our body. When our body is in healthy harmony we are more able to focus on our spiritual, mental and emotional needs.

Let's respect our health and develop a daily maintenance program that will carry us joyfully into the years ahead; lovingly care for this God given temple. You'll be amazed at what a big difference even the smallest adjustment in your diet and fitness routine can make.

A recent Duke University study found that loneliness and depression are the most common triggers of overeating in women. Exercise, which lifts the spirit as it burns the fat, can help to eliminate the blues. A brisk walk, a bike ride or a game of tennis can do wonders. Psychologists also suggest turning to a wise friend instead of comfort foods; and talking out your anxiety can make you feel better. Tackle problems without the help of food. Try not to eat when you are feeling stressed. Sip a cup of herbal tea with honey, do some deep breathing exercises or take a warm bath to calm your nerves and help you feel more in control.

Have a good breakfast. It will help curb your appetite for the rest of the day and get your metabolism moving. Try getting up fifteen minutes earlier to enjoy a delicious breakfast. Pour apple juice over breakfast cereal instead of whole milk. For home-made muffins use applesauce in place of butter or oil in baking; or replace butter on toast with jelly. Studies show fueling-up with complex carbohydrates, such as whole grain breads, fresh fruits, and cereal within two hours of rising will help you burn five percent more calories all day.

Have healthy foods and snacks within your reach. Keep a bowl of cool grapes in the refrigerator; cut-up raw vegetables in containers, or munch on fat-free whole grain pretzels. Healthful food gives you an energy lift. Opt for fresh fruit rather than juice. A piece of fruit takes longer to consume and makes you feel fuller because it is loaded with fiber. Plus, it is lower in calories than fruit juice.

Experts recommend that you do at least a half hour of moderate aerobic activity at least three times a week for instant calorie burning, plus toning exercises to keep your metabolism primed.

Make meal times special. Arrange fresh flowers on the table, listen to soothing music, and use pretty dishes. Listening to slow music during dinner can make you take smaller bites, chew longer and eat slower. When you eat, don't watch TV, read, or pay bills. Focus on having a great meal or talking with your family or friends. Savor each bite.

Clear the table as soon as you're finished to keep from sitting around and picking when you are no longer hungry. Ask your family to help you put away extra food after your meal so you won't be tempted to pick at all the leftovers.

Remember the color rule. Fill your plate with colorful foods. The more colors on your plate, the more nutrients you are probably getting. Green beans, corn, tomatoes, carrots, beets. Get the picture?

For a chocolate craving, fat-free chocolate syrup can be your saving grace. Drizzle it on yogurt or fresh fruit for a delicious dessert or try a nonfat chocolate sorbet.

Stop eating at least three hours before bedtime so you eliminate fat storage while you sleep. Then, when you wake-up, you are ready for a healthful breakfast. Eat dinner early; between five and six o'clock. Group studies concluded that those who ate the same number of calories earlier gained less and slept better.

Don't punish yourself if you have one bad eating day. Reflect on your accomplishments and reward yourself for your fitness victories. Experience the joy of each precious day. This will affirm that a fulfilling life does not focus on food. Find the strength to overcome any obstacles that hinder your stamina. Increase your self confidence, inner strength and discipline by ending your day with a word of thanks to your loving, heavenly Father.

Relax and Think Deep Thoughts

"Take quiet moments throughout the day for your own enjoyment and peace of mind"

A serene face will show far fewer wrinkles than one that has spent years on reacting to a constant diet of stress and tension. We must learn to relax and take quiet moments throughout the day just for our enjoyment and peace of mind.

In times of tranquillity, we have a chance to rest, an opportunity to evaluate our lives and gain valuable insight. A chance to appreciate our wellbeing, our dreams and the unlimited possibilities of the future, a realization of a higher purpose of our lives.

It is a commendable practice to have daily quiet time. Follow relaxation techniques such as deep breathing and meditation to help you relax. Try forgetting everything and completely relaxing your mind. Keep your thoughts off of the elements which weaken our lives and fix your mind on the good and positive things in your life. Cast out all resentment, fear and anxiety. Replace these feelings with faith, love and hope, through which great and wonderful things can happen.

Here are ways that you can begin to unwind and cloth yourself in serenity.

- Visualization. Imagine yourself in a relaxing scene. Close your eyes and picture a tranquil, peaceful setting. Use all of your senses. Feel the warmth of the sun, smell the lily in the field, and hear the soothing sound of the trees rustling in the breeze.
- Pet Therapy. Hugging your cat or dog can reduce stress. Snuggling with a soft and fuzzy kitten or puppy can soothe your worries. Pets can enrich our lives and give unconditional love.
- Escape. Take a leisurely stroll by the shoreline. Listen to the waves crashing on the rocks, read a book by your favorite author or collect seashells. A sense of calmness can come over you as you escape from your present environment for an hour or two.
- Yoga. This involves the holding of stretches and poses often combined with breathing exercises. This can reduce mental fatigue, lower blood pressure and encourages you to breath more deeply and slowly. You can purchase a video tape or enroll in a class.
- Have a massage. A massage therapist can knead tense muscles. This can also have a calming effect of the central nervous system.
- Set aside time to pray. God also set aside a day of rest. Focus on the blessings and promises that God has given. Remember other people in your prayers. Let the serenity of your "New You" overflow and spill out into the lives of others.

And as Henry David Thoreau described, "It is something to be able to paint a lovely portrait, or to carve a magnificent statue, but it is far more glorious to carve and paint the very atmosphere in which we live."

As you live life, your values, your sense of identity and inner-direction will infuse exhilaration and peace.

Wisdom's Call

"Your ears may hear the sound of the rain but wisdom knows the storm will pass"

There is a tinge of chill in the air as fall comes upon us again. The trees are aflame with color, the aroma of apple pie baking in the oven and the evening is aglow with the romance of a full harvest moon.

Autumn brings the night echoes, as the crickets bid farewell. Squirrels gather their nuts to prepare for winter and the great oak trees hide life saving sap deep in their roots. Nature, in all its magnificent splendor, heeds the call of Wisdom.

These precious days and golden hours hold for you and I the miracle of life and the priceless jewels of wisdom. Gaining wisdom is more valuable than gold or silver. Be sensitive to wisdom's call. Listen closely and carefully.

As with nature, we can find wisdom in unexpected places. Events that we have experienced, people who inspire us, and from the instruction of trusted friends. A stream of wisdom is often the result of choppy waves and rough seas. Our greatest lessons can often be the most painful. But through these difficulties, you can acquire great knowledge. The worst thing that you go through may turn out to be your richest blessing. "All things work together for good, to those who love God." –Romans 8:28. Your ears may hear the sound of the rain, but wisdom knows the storm will pass.

Wisdom grows out of a lifetime of experience, but also can be learned from the most innocent child. Do not store up your wisdom, share it with mankind. Help others with the wisdom and knowledge that has helped you. The advice of a teacher, grandparent or mentor can be a rich source of guidance. A wise person takes heed to advice and accepts instruction. “He who walks with the wise, grows wise, but a companion of fools suffers harm.” –Proverbs 13:20. The unforgettable testimonies of the wise and their experiences can give you insight for the future. History can repeat itself in your life.

Biblical wisdom offers comfort; tremendous depth can add great meaning to your daily life. The literature in the Bible holds secrets of true success and happiness. Infuse your wisdom with God’s presence. The spiritual dimensions of wisdom enriches the relationship between you and God. Great inner peace comes from a close bond with Him. Wisdom is as close as asking and praying.

You may not get an immediate answer to some of your prayers. The reason may not be clear right away, but sooner or later, it will be as plain as day. I’m sure you have seen this amazing power work out in your own life, when you planned and prayed desperately. Then, looking back, you shudder, when you think what would have happened if your request had been granted. Miraculous wisdom, far greater than your own, was at work. What if you had married that person who would have never made you happy, took that job in another city with a company that soon folded or won a million dollars that would have torn your family apart. Yes, you were disappointed at the time, but now you are so thankful that God has more joyous plans for you and greater treasures. When you seek Him you will understand many mysteries and experience a genuine happiness that only a relationship with Him can bring. Feel God’s presence and know that He is there to help, strengthen and guide you to a long and fulfilling life.

Be as wise as the trees. Guard your dreams of life deep in your heart from the cold blast of unbelief. Be like the squirrels and in wisdom, store up the food of God’s word in your life to carry you to victory. Be like the stars that hold steady in their courses; stick to your goals. All nature listens to wisdom’s call.

Happy Valley – What is Happiness?

" Get in to the habit of looking on the sunny side of each situation you encounter."

The happiest people don't necessarily have the best of everything, they just make the best of everything. William Branham said, "Character is not a gift, it's a victory," and Dwight Eisenhower said, "There are no victories at bargain prices." We are not meant to be wishy-washy people, we are to fight like good soldiers.

Happy people all have their share of problems, disappointments and adversity. But they know the dark times won't last and they FOCUS on bringing forth the beauty and joy out of every situation. Every obstacle presents an opportunity to improve one's conditions. Accept the valleys, they occur in every life. But remember, the Bible says, "By sorrow the heart is made better." Believe that yours will be made better in each valley. You and only you govern the thoughts that enter your mind.

As a true soldier, give every ounce of your strength to break the enemy's hold on depressing your emotions. Push those negative thoughts out of your mind, fight until you win and plant the flag of victorious promises in place everyday. If you have to, put little notes of inspiration on your bathroom mirror, the dashboard of your car, on your desk or on the refrigerator.

Giving out to others faith, charity, honesty, sincerity, hope and love will result in happiness. These qualities will endure and can provide you with peace of mind and harmony within your soul. Love is the strongest force in the world, so love and respect all people. Envy no one. You don't know their hidden sorrows. Keep gossip away from your lips. Words are only worth speaking when they improve and uplift the hearer. And believe me, positive words spoken give strength and uplifts the bearer.

Appreciate all that you have, the intangible riches that you now possess. Your life is a special gift born from the goodness of God. Wake up and say "thank you" for this brand new day. Don't be preoccupied with tomorrow's worries; appreciate today. We always have something to be thankful for. Remember the story about the man who was upset because he had no shoes until he met a man with no feet.

"Goodness is the only investment that never fails," said Thoreau.

The more you share the more you will have. There are small opportunities that surround us everyday to help and support our fellow human beings. A friend of mine always says, "I'm really the happiest when I am doing something for someone else." Sincere concern for the lonely, the poor or a next door neighbor can take you out of yourself into the joy of compassionate caring. Life is like a mirror, it reflects back what you put into it.

You can attract the happiness you desire by filling your mind, heart and soul with positive thoughts, prayer and thankfulness. Make up your mind to be happy. Get into the habit of looking on the sunny side of each situation you encounter. The slothful person who does nothing to change is miserable.

Let us act as the happiest person does; the one who fights the battle all day long and plants the flag of victory on a mountaintop each night. There we are closer to God and sleep the sweet sleep of the victor. In the morning, we awake in the strength and power of God's thoughts. And walk on higher ground, letting the light of the Son fill our whole being, for His light shines in the lowest valleys and on the highest heights and on the triumphant soldier in battle.

The Master Mind

*"Anything you put your mind to do...
you can do"*

Albert Einstein, one of the greatest scientists and mathematicians that the world had ever known, was born of ordinary parents. Einstein was an average student with limited formal education. Before he died, he willed his brain to medical science. The best scientists in the nation carefully studied it. Their report? Einstein was average in every way. No unusual characteristics or additional matter. For all practical purposes, identical to the brain of any other man of Einstein's age.

The difference between you and the "world's greatest genius" was that Einstein became so fascinated by mathematics that he devoted every spare minute and the entire power of his mind to its mastery. All successful achievement begins in your mind. Anything you set your mind to do, you can do.

The mind is the controlling tower of the whole body. It directs us, controls our thoughts and our actions. Every person is what their dominating thoughts are in their mind. "Whether you think you can or you think you can't, you're right," wrote Henry Ford.

Translate your plans into action. Write down your goals. Make a list, in order of importance, of the things you really want. Goal setting is one of the strongest forces for human motivation. Once you have put your goal in writing, you have made a commitment to make it come true. The instruments Einstein used to develop intricate and profound theories regarding the universe and the natural laws that control it were a pencil and paper. He wrote down his questions, ideas and answers. Put your plans and ideas on paper. Make notes of all creative thoughts that come into your mind. Only the ones who plan it out are the ones who succeed. Decide what you want.

Speak aloud your goals. Your words are powerful. By confessing the things you desire and believing in your heart they will come to pass, your mind will begin the creative process that will help you to achieve your objective. You can have what you say. Continually affirm your goals. Your body obeys the command of the mind. Repeat those positive words over and over again. Vivid pictures in your mind become a reality.

Take action. Once you decide what you want, act upon your decision. Do it now! Success is waiting to happen. What you make of your life is all up to you.

Eliminate extra baggage. Rid yourself of everything that hinders your success. These entanglements keep us from being all that we can be and pulls strength out of us. Cast aside all negativity. Isolate yourself from individuals who discourage you. The people who try to knock you down are only trying to reduce you to their size.

Form new habits, a positive outlook and a winning attitude. Make yourself over in your mind. Be positive, it is the key to success in every situation. Life is certain to bring disappointment, but in spite of it all, with the help of God, you can be an overcomer. His promotions often come in the disguise of failure.

Every person was born with a gift; it is your individual treasure and your calling in life. I believe in great success and know that it is ours, without a doubt, by keeping our hearts in tune with each other and in constant communication with the Master's Mind.

Hard Work and Patience Will Be Rewarded

"God's delays are not God's denials"

The Wright Brothers went through tremendous trouble on their way to success. It took nine years of trials and mostly errors before the Wright Brothers were able to make a plane that could fly.

What can keep a person going year after year, day after day, moving toward a dream without giving up? The Wright Brothers practiced the art of faith and patience.

There is no great accomplishment that is not the result of hard work, patience, and trying, trying again. The more enduring your patience, the more certain your reward. God's delays are not God's denials.

Anything of value takes time. "Learn to labor and to wait," said Longfellow. Everything unfolds at its own pace and in its natural course. You never can tell how close you are to your goal. When it seems so far away, take another step; it may be right around the corner.

Prepare while you wait, so when opportunity knocks, you will be ready. Most people quit too soon. Do not give up if you face a temporary setback. When Thomas Edison invented the light bulb, he tried over 2000 experiments before he got one to work. Rise up if you fall and have the patience and courage to try again.

Walk slowly toward your goal with steadfast faith. Don't be deterred. Wisdom knows that there is no swift journey to success. Avoid anything that offers you a quick ride to the top. Patience can be bitter at times, but when you achieve your goals the fruit will be so sweet.

Patience is power. It has been said that patience is a virtue, and virtue means strength. Patience is the best remedy for trouble. Time heals all wounds. It is the ability to bear affliction with calmness and confidence and an inward peace, as well as outward control. Patience can carry us through difficult times.

Enjoy each day while on the path to your goals. The journey itself can be most exciting. Happiness is having a life filled with expectation. Orville Wright wrote in his diary, "Each day is filled with a sense of discoveries waiting to be made. Wilber and I could hardly wait for morning to come to get to something that interested us." The road to your goals can be packed with as much joy as the final destination will be. Do not rush through life. Patience can allow us to experience fully what is happening now, at this very moment, even if we have an eye on the future.

Keep your goal in sight. When the reward is visible, patience comes more easily. There is a season, a place and a time for everything. Relish your wonderful life now. Have a strong faith and a heart that know that with time and patience your dreams will unfold before your eyes.

I believe that God rewards the patient and persistent person. He has good reason for every delay that He allows to come our way. God has great plans for you; in His perfect time, He will reveal them all. All of a sudden, the day of success is here... the reward of patience has come. You will fly, like the Wright brothers, over a smoke-screen of impossibility.

Crowns of Simplicity

"Choose to be rich by making your wants few"

It is the glory of God to conceal the matter. Our Lord has hidden an abundance of pure, lovely and sparkling jewels in simplicity. And with a simple life comes old-fashioned joys, peace of mind and a satisfaction within your heart. All this and more is found in a clean, honest and simple life.

The most beautiful jewel in the world is a life lived harmoniously and unencumbered. We must be free of owning too many things so that they do not own us. The greatest blessings in life are already within you or certainly within your reach. These are the things that cannot be taken away or purchased with money. Choose to be rich by making your wants few. Desire only three things. As the years unfold, we want to carry with us precious treasures of: 1. Happy Memories 2. True Friendships 3. Sterling Character.

❦ Create happy memories. Be aware each day of the beauty and splendor that surrounds you. The glorious autumn colors that were painted by God's artistic hand, a breathtaking sunrise and the smile of a child. Pick apples with a friend, sit at an outdoor cafe or go window-shopping. Take a nature walk and come home feeling refreshed. Place cherished family pictures in a scrapbook with a personal or humorous written comment by each photo, so you can look back on happy moments and reminisce. Put fresh flowers in your home and smell their sweet fragrance. Build a swing for your porch, go on a picnic or take a drive by the shoreline and listen to the crashing of the waves. Live your life at an easy pace. Savor each moment and every hour. Slow down and remind yourself of the natural order of things.

- Nourish true friendships. With a true friend, life can be full of joy and happiness. Cultivate peace of mind to be used as a power center out of which comes an abundance of energy for social living. Use wisdom concerning choosing who you spend your time with and curtail demands that others put on your life. Only be with those people who you truly trust and love. Say, "no" to the things that you do not want to do, true friends will respect your decisions. Simplify your life by putting a filter over your ears. Filter or block out anything that is negative. If someone starts to gossip, stop them in their tracks. Simply say, "I don't want to hear it." A friend will honor that. Be there for friends in sunshine or in a shadow.
- Achieve sterling character. Character is not a gift, it is a victory. Against all obstacles, appreciate your life with a thankful heart. Spend the first five minutes of your day in thanksgiving and gratitude to God. His love is steadfast, faithful and endless. Have some quiet time each day to feel God's presence. Share a smile and it will give those around you a lift. At work, be diligent, honest and courteous, showing respect to your co-workers. At home, talk openly and sincerely with your spouse. Create a space of tranquillity in your home, a little area where you can go to pray, read or write. Practice joyful acts of love. Anonymously, put a plant on a friends doorstep, visit a shut-in or help others in the best way you can.

There is such beauty in simplicity. By devoting my best to develop these three priorities, God has touched my life with grace. These small revelations have a way of expanding into great joy that makes life worth living and celebrating. This is God's crowning gift to us.

God's Shining Light Streams Into Your Garden

"Just as the Master Gardener gave to us, lets in turn, help others reap a rich crop."

You are the caretaker of a beautiful garden in a magnificent, grand estate. Many have traveled from distant lands to witness the beauty and splendor of the garden. Thousands of glorious flowers cover the land. Each lovely petal was selected and placed with gentle care. Acres of blossoms, in brilliant hues from the palest yellow, to vibrant pinks and deep red, fill your garden a superb display of God's creation. Waterfalls cascading down through the landscape, designed by your hands.

As your garden grows, behold the majesty of nature and the mysteries of life. Days pass, seasons change and months melt into years. As we look at our gardens, the childhood memories, cherished traditions and renowned enthusiasm enlarge our hearts and give us increased wisdom. Your garden is a masterpiece in many colors and restores itself with each season. Within each of us lies this garden. The garden is in our hearts.

Like ivy on the stone walls, our lives and the lives of others are inescapably entwined. When we plant the seeds of love in other's lives, we reap a harvest of love in our own hearts. For goodness returns and is multiplied. Each act of kindness represents a flower's full bloom. Reach out with compassion to one another. Just as the Master Gardener gave to us, let's in turn, help others reap a rich crop.

Allow God's sunlight to stream through your garden. Feel the warmth, the peace and the tranquillity of His great simplicity. Uncomplicate your life. The simpler your life, the more peaceful it will be.

To quench the thirst of the garden, you must water it. Truth is the water that washes away the bareness of the ground. A summer's day can suddenly turn into an angry storm. But, the storms of life don't have to get inside of us. Paint the walls of your mind with beautiful pictures. At the end of the storm, make a rainbow appear. God doesn't take us through troubled waters to drown us, He takes us there to strengthen us.

Make your life blossom. Let your dreams take hold, even through adversity. When the cold winter comes, perennial dreams will survive. Once again, they rise up, the leaves unfurl and flowers bloom. Each year do more. Plant as many dreams as you can and you will continue to grow.

Use caution in whom you trust. Impostors can tear up your crop of dreams. Be careful of the subtly of the serpent. Guard your heart. The serpent's wrong thoughts, actions and attitude can come disguised in a very attractive package. And, if left to remain, the serpent can destroy all of the loveliness of the garden.

Be watchful of your garden when it begins to flourish. It is at that exact time when the serpents will come. Your magnificent masterpiece is much too precious to end up in ruin. Shield your garden. God will help you. Remember, no matter how deeply the serpent wounds, the Master Gardener can heal and repair. He will take care of His own.

In the landscape of our lives, with every passing day we learn that the Master Gardener is the One who is in control. With His protection, you can create beauty in your life as you care for the garden in your heart.

God Has a Plan for the Life of Every Person

"You are precious and are esteemed the most valuable treasure on earth."

The One who formed the brilliant stars and made the vast oceans created you out of His great love. His genuine devotion to His children lights the way as we travel through life.

God's love is sincere and constant and knows no boundaries or limits. Just as each star has its place and course, God has given to each of us a divine purpose, a plan for our lives.

As your guide, He will take you out of confusion and will help you to reach your destiny.

You are a worthwhile, significant and valuable person. Since the beginning of time, there has never been anyone else exactly like you and there never will be again. There is no one that can duplicate all of the attributes that only you possess. You are precious and are esteemed; the most valuable treasure on earth. Generously equipped in both mind and body, you can do miraculous things with your life. You have extraordinary capabilities and the world can benefit from your many talents. Utilize your full potential to make the world a better place for yourself and for generations to follow. Everyone has many gifts to offer; find what you are best at and give that gift to others.

Have a healthy self respect. God made you very special, so hold a high opinion of your own worth. Exude an air of gentle confidence. People will perceive you, as you perceive yourself. Gentleness is not an absence of power, but a sign of great inner strength. How you act will determine how people will react to you. Self-confidence differs from conceit or arrogance; it is a calm, serenely poised attitude that dares to achieve the very best.

Do not be afraid. Every noble acquisition has its risk. But, you can adjust to any challenge or hardship if you have a sincerity to overcome. Shake off any mistakes of the day. God gives you new opportunities each morning.

This life is your constant opportunity. Create your own special dreams. Never be convinced that your goals are too high. Let others dig a cave, you can build a castle! As a child of God, you too deserve the best, nothing is too good for you. Be what you dream to be and make your life everything you always hoped for.

You have complete control over the choices you make, so use wisdom. Choose respect not ruthlessness. Make sure your choices will benefit not only yourself, but others as well, and your success will be sweet.

Do not listen to those who try to demean you. There will be some who will be jealous of you and who will try to distract you from your dreams. Be strong. Never allow another person to rob you from doing your best to achieve your goals. Believe in yourself... I believe in you.

Just as each star is distinct and one of a kind, so are you. This life is your occasion to shine. So, give out your own radiant light, encouraging and inspiring others, while sharing joy and promise. This is the dawning of a new day and "A New You."

The Choice – a Powerful Privilege

"You have the power over your own destiny and the freedom to live your life in any way in which you choose."

There are an infinite number of choices to make in your lifetime. Where to live, a life's companion and raising children, to name a few. Your way of life is by far the most crucial choice. The way that you choose to live and your attitude that you choose to live by are the most important decisions you will ever make.

As a creation of God, we each have been given the opportunity to create our own circumstances. Rejoice in the knowledge that you have the power over your own destiny and the freedom to live your life in any way in which you choose.

Listen closely to your inner voice. That voice that will guide you through many of life's most difficult decisions. Trust your inner resources. Carefully listen to your inner self and follow through with what it tells you. God gave us all a conscience that is very sensitive and disconcerting. Your inner person will sometimes grasp a situation or personality before your outer consciousness ever perceives it.

Be strong enough to be confident in your choices once they are made. We all have to confront hard issues from time to time, but conflicts and struggles strengthen us and mold our character. I believe that things always work out for the best. You will never be asked to bear more than you can cope with. Crises tap into powers that you didn't know were there and actually make you a better, wiser and stronger person than you ever were before.

The choices that make a significant difference in our lives can be the toughest. These decisions are not easy by any means. Rely on your own knowledge of what is right. Trust yourself, your dreams and you intuitions. Have faith and assurance that your inner voice will guide you to the life that will bring you the most happiness and fulfillment.

Choose to form good habits. The power of choosing good over bad is within all of us. Your future and the future of those who love you depends on your choices. If you do the right things, good things will happen. We control our destiny and making the right decisions will contribute to our future.

Choose to live a healthy lifestyle. Eat right and exercise daily. Stay away from drugs and alcohol. These addictions can kill you. Keep your mind busy planning to do the things that you desire. Utilize your time wisely and make every day count. Redirect your life if you have to. You have the choice. No one can make you change, you must be willing to help yourself. There are many wonderful organizations ready to help those in need.

Fill your time with creative choices. Do the things that will help you grow as a person. Keep yourself vibrantly alive. Enroll in a book club, go hiking in the woods, attend a crafts fair or volunteer your time to a local hospital. All that you do should reflect your own style, passion and love.

Have confidence in your choices and choose to live your life as beautifully as possible.

Moments of Renewal

"Take a minute now to slow down, take a deep breath and savor life more completely."

The rush, hustle and bustle of life seems so frantic lately, it feels good just to sit here quietly in isolation and do nothing. Though my mind races at a record high speed , as I'm sure yours does, on the 20 plus things I must get done before tomorrow, I find it suddenly very important to take time out for soothing moments of sacred quietness.

Life can become so intense, we feel there is just not enough hours in a day, juggling families, careers, chores, etc. This inner stress can make you ill. So give yourself permission to enjoy the peace and tranquillity of seclusion – moments of renewal. There is an enemy who wants to speed things up and put a whole bunch of problems in our path, like the waving arms of a basketball guard, so we feel overwhelmed, confused and don't know which way to turn. But, we have a choice to stop for a second, turn around from all that stress and negativity and make our goal.

Take a minute now to slow down, take a deep breath and savor life more completely. An opportunity to heal the body and quiet the soul – to bring balance and harmony into your heart once again. Taking time out is the best cure for stress. Think of quiet intervals in the day as a long term investment in your peace of mind and quality of life. If you are experiencing anxiety, take a break from whatever is causing you the pressure. It's o.k. to do nothing, to spend an afternoon alone. "Life moves pretty quick, if you don't stop and look around once in a while you could miss it," says a reader. Bring a tea tray outdoors, a bowl of cool grapes and an inviting book to regroup, be calm and still. Sit back passively and observe the restorative beauty of creation. Behold the majesty of the glorious world that God created for our pleasure. Nature is like a form of medication that acts as a healing balm over your entire being.

Take solitude in the morning, before the beginning of the day or perhaps it would be more convenient in the evening, after the children have gone to sleep. Schedule your quiet time and adhere to it. In quietness and confidence you possess your soul. In silence you can collect your thoughts and ideas. Even Presidents and Generals go to Camp David to take a day or weekend to be at peace and think.

We become too much creatures of time. To God there is no time. So, lets walk with Him for a little bit each day. His peace surpasses all the substitutes the world has to offer. Being alone can give your creative spirit a chance to recoup. Idleness is not always uncreative.

What can be more idle than sleep. But, God has made us so we must take in a certain amount of hours to sleep and be still, so we will be refreshed and restored for the day that lies ahead. When we are asleep, we are unconscious of that restoration, but He also made us so we could take moments of quietness when we are awake and be wise enough to take in His thoughts and restore our minds to right thinking.

Nighttime is beginning to fall and the misty earth is starting to turn a pearl gray. The sky is brushed with amethyst and the setting sun edges the clouds with pure gold.

As dusk nears, the sound of cooing doves and the sweet chirps of a birds last lingering bits of praise soothe our souls.

It feels as though God is so near. How lovingly, gently and peacefully, He puts the world to sleep. Like a mother, pulling a down comforter over her new born baby, so the Lord pulls a blanket of night clouds over us. This evening will give us a chance to rest, to be refreshed and rejuvenated for the glorious day that awaits us tomorrow.

The Season of Rebirth

"Let us create harmony in our homes, our businesses and in the lives of others."

Every year, the whole of nature gives witness to the resurrection of life. The miraculous season of rebirth. Tulips bloom and crocuses lift their heads, daffodils, jonquil's, and sweet smelling narcissus come forth out of the apparently barren Mother earth. Trees announce with promising buds their fullness to come. The Easter Lily looks like a pure, white angel trumpet declaring the glory of the resurrection of new life and that all things shall live again.

Let us consider spring as we have never considered it before, taking it personally into our hearts and becoming one with its promise. It symbolizes that no matter how you lived before, you can have a rebirth where your whole spirit is fresh and new. Be at peace with this joyous time of the singing birds, velvet grass, butterflies, and nodding flowers. Let God's love warm you like rays of sunshine enveloping all.

Oh, how I yearn to plant blossoms upon blossoms of these heaven sent beauties in my garden, delicate lilies of the valley, pretty pansies, and violets. Every little innocent flower will breathe God's love back to me. With a light breeze their love will flow right back into my waiting soul. As the tightly closed bud feels the warmth of the sun and begins to open, turn your thoughts to God's word and feel the warmth of His life and love to make you a new creation. You can look at any flower, tree or sunset and see your Father in Heaven. Everything He created tells us something about Him. He is tender and precious, majestic and beautiful. All that we create tells something about us. Let us create harmony in our homes, our businesses and in the lives of others.

We all have been through trials and heartaches that left us feeling like the barren branches of the winter's chill. But as we search deep in our hearts, way down deep as the trees' sap, we will find hidden the spark of precious new life. Even if we have to go as far back as little children and be reminded of the sweet song, "Jesus loves me… this, I know, for the Bible tells me so…" God is hidden in simplicity. Bring that little song up from the depth of your soul, to your heart, up to a mouth to sing it and eyes to shine it forth. Repeat precious inspiring words again and again until they drop from your mind into your heart, then they have become a part of a new you. Like a reader wrote, "When I read your column it was so comforting I cut it out of the paper and laminated it. I read it over and over again." Blossoming, like a beautiful flower, let our arms and hands show deeds of love. God's love never fails. His mercies are new every morning. With child-like faith, lift up your arms like the branches of the trees and praise God that another spring has been given. Let us make the resurrection of life be more apparent in our hearts than the world we see around us. Begin to react to the warm love light of the Creator and He will give you new life. Stir up your mind to consider Him, your mouth to speak His love and your heart to know that you are of great value to Him; more precious than diamonds and rubies.

Come alive again this spring. With your whole being, turn and embrace all of God's promises especially this one, "Behold, I make all things new." Let the transforming love of this Easter be the beginning of a new creation, "A New You."

Fun Has No Age Limit!

"Help your grandchild or neighbors child make a lemonade stand. And be sure to be the first paying customer."

I have a wonderful, creative friend who is full of fun. She is 57 years old and last month she and her son built a tree house for her 6-year-old grandson. This wonderful creation has a spiral staircase with a railing of small branches going up around the tree trunk. Then came the floor, walls half wood and half screen, and finally the roof. Up on a side limb there is a "look out" tower, plus a rope to swing on. The tree top dwelling can hold ten children or five adults comfortably. The grand opening was on her grandson's birthday and they held a cookout and roasted hotdogs for family and friends. As the sun set, the tree house shook with children's laughter and magically she flipped a switch and the whole spiral staircase and marvelous tree house was outlined in little white lights. Enchanting fun for both children and adults. Later, her 32-year-old son and grandson slept in the tree house, telling stories under the shining stars. They awakened to the spreading light of dawn and the joyful song of the birds. For breakfast, my wondrous friend filled a basket with hot pancakes, syrup, and bacon in tight plastic containers; she packed small cartons of orange juice, paper plates and plastic forks, then called up to the tree house, "Lower the rope maties." Tying the breakfast basket onto the rope, her grandson hauled it up into the tree house. The delighted "oohs and aahs" of boy and man as they dug into the goodies was music to her ears.

There is only one word to describe such excitement and frolic… Summer!

There is no age limit on fun, so whatever age you may be there is fun awaiting you! Just take your pick:

- Plan a picnic and find a favorite park bench to sit on. Feed and make friends with the squirrels and ducks.
- Build a playhouse for a special daughter or granddaughter. Wallpaper the walls, put lace curtains on the windows and hang tiny pictures. Hold a house warming for her friends and bake hot cookies. Only three at a time inside and as many as you want outside sitting on pretty quilts. The world is full of great fun to discover.
- Make a tiny backyard pool. Dig a hole about a foot deep and as large as you want. Buy a plastic drop cloth at the dollar store and line the pool. Cover the edges with rocks and fill it up with water. Get some gold fish and plant a rock garden around the rim of the pool with flowers and mosses.
- Camp out in the backyard. Pitch a tent, get some sleeping bags and build a campfire. Toast marshmallows, sing songs and make smores. You remember smores, made of two graham crackers, with a marshmallow, and a piece of chocolate in between, toasted over the fire in a hamburger holder…yum, yum.
- Make your garden special. Visit a nursery and pick out some beautiful plants and flowers. Make little signs such as, "You're nearer to God's heart in a garden." Then, find a birdbath and make a sign for our feathered friends that says, "Free baths…this way."

- Enjoy an ice-cream cone on a hot summer's evening at a local ice-cream shop or make your own cool treats at home by investing in a good old-fashioned ice cream maker.
- Go to a minor or major league baseball game and be sure to stand up and cheer for your team.
- Help your grandchild or neighbors child make a lemonade stand. And be sure to be the first paying customer.
- Stargaze. On a clear night lie on a big, fluffy blanket. Sip sparkling cider and snack on fresh fruit, crackers and cheese. Look upon the heavens and know that you have a heavenly Father who delights in your fun and happiness.

There's an old saying, "that you don't get any older while you're fishing." Young or old, summer promises days of delight for all the very young at heart.

The Greatest Gifts I Can Give

"My beloved child, you are a miracle as every child is."

We walked into the room that will soon be your nursery. Your daddy and I just finished shopping for your canopy crib, so beautiful in pure white.

Your daddy carefully pats my tummy and says, "I love you baby…" I know you can hear his words and recognize his gentle voice. This is one of the wonderful reasons why I married him… I knew he would be a loving, kind and caring father.

Through all the joyous preparations and plans we hold in our hearts something much more valuable, our love for you.

My beloved child, you are a miracle as every child is. With each passing day, I feel your presence and anticipate your arrival.

I'll always remember that evening, after the sun set and the gorgeous colors were woven into a tapestry across the sky and the twilight shadows fell, I came back into your sweet nursery. The soft glow of the moon came streaming into the window when suddenly, and without even realizing it, I was on my knees. Hands folded and praying to the good Lord that He will help and guide your father and I to give you the gifts that really matter. "My child, give me your heart, and let your eyes observe my ways." –Proverbs 23:26.

- Can we teach you to have faith? By believing and having faith you can bring forth all the greatness in yourself. God will always make a way where there is no way.
- Can we teach you to count your blessings? Always be thankful for what you have.
- Can we teach you follow your dreams? With persistence and determination you can achieve anything. With ordinary talent and extraordinary perseverance all things are attainable. Everyone makes mistakes; they will teach you valuable lessons.
- Can we teach you to respect and learn from nature? There are miracles are all around you. What can be more miraculous than a caterpillar turning into a butterfly or an egg into a chick? Relish all the beauty that God created for your enjoyment.
- Can we teach you to cope with difficulties? Things may not always be easy, but it is from adversity that strength is born. To try to look on the bright side of each situation and to trust in God.
- Can we teach you good moral values – characteristics such as honesty and fairness?
- Can we teach you that you can be anything you want in life as long as you work hard and are willing to pay a price to reach your goals? Take pride in your work.
- Can we teach you not to be afraid? To be courageous and do what is right? Do not worry, dear child, there is no fear in love.

- Can we teach you to pray? God will help you with any task or solve any problem if you let Him. Delight in Him and He will give you your hearts desire and will direct your path.
- Can we teach you to love everyone, to be open-minded and see each person as a child of God? Share with others, giving positive words of kindness, helping a neighbor and having compassion for the less fortunate.
- Can we teach you to live life to the fullest? Life is a precious gift. Share your wonderful, unique qualities with the world, to think, to create, to imagine and to believe. Know that you are valuable, a child of God and worthy of every good thing.

Yes, we can… for we can do all things through Christ who strengthens us.

And when I look into my child's tender face for the very first time and he or she looks into mine, that exchange of looks I will carry with me all of my life. And the greatest gift I can give to you, my child, will be to know that God lives in your heart and that your mommy and daddy love you so, so much.

Redeeming Love and Heavenly Habits

"The smallest gesture makes a difference when it is done from the heart."

I sometimes wonder what God thinks or how He feels when He witnesses people being unkind to one another. A tear must come to His eye and it must sadden Him deeply for He loves us so much. His joy is for us to be happy. And He knows our truest happiness is found in serving Him and loving others.

Let us take each other's hand and bit by bit, and little by little, make the world a better place. A universe filled with what God had intended...His children living in harmony, love and good will. How do we do this? First and above all, show your appreciation to God by loving and showering kindness to fellow human beings. Begin to show these little gems of graciousness, gentleness and compassion to those you come into contact with daily. The smallest gesture makes a difference when it is done from the heart. It can mean as much to the recipient as the grandest, most expensive jewel.

"You must give time to your fellow men, even if it's a little thing. Do something for others. Something for which you get no pay, but the privilege of doing it." –Albert Schewitzer.

"Only a life lived for others is worth living." –Albert Einstein.

"Living for others is a sign of eternal life." –William Branham.

So, lets begin living the way we will for eternity and form these heavenly habits:

- The joy of the Lord is our strength, so develop a sense of humor and make a lonely person laugh.
- With celestial grace, stop for a moment and hold the door open for the person behind you. Not only take a bouquet of flowers to a patient in a hospital, but sit down, hold their hand and say a prayer with them for a quick recovery.
- Repay unkindness with kindness. Goodness will always overcome evil. Your life will become so meaningful, so important. Let go of an old grudge. Bless those who persecute you. Forgiveness makes a happy heart.
- Give God the creator great respect and keep the land beautiful, never litter.
- As angels are everywhere helping us, find creative ways to help in your community.
- Our heavenly Father touches hearts simultaneously all over the world, so call a friend who lives out of town just to say, "I love you" and let them know that you're thinking about them.
- Take your sweet natured pets on visits to the local nursing home. You can make a profound impact in someone's life by helping those in need. With every deed you are sowing a seed, though the harvest you may not yet see.
- Give a compliment, a smile and a word of praise to those you meet along the way. Stress the positive. Say something especially nice to the checkout person at the grocery store. Offer to carry an older persons groceries to his or her car.
- Hug your spouse. Give each other that extra-special attention and time every day. "Don't let the sun set on an argument," suggests a reader. "If you have a difference in opinion, patch it up that night."

Kindness is the golden chain by which we are bound together. Spread the joy of the Lord where ever you may go. Live in His peace and good will. Look up to the heavens and rest upon the Lord, with a thankful heart, at the beginning of each miraculous day. Our heavenly habits will make Him so happy!

The Beauty Remains

"Your true beauty, like Renoir's painting is timeless and becomes more valuable with age"

Auguste Renoir was almost paralyzed by arthritis. When the great artist was asked why he continued to paint when he was in such agony, Renoir replied, "The beauty remains, the pain passes."

Your true beauty will not pass with pain or sorrow. It will remain, as long as you have love in your heart, thankfulness on your lips, encouragement for others and hope for the future. You must take special care of your inner-self, for beauty is more, much more than skin deep... it radiates from your unique and wonderful personality.

It's important to take care of yourself so you feel your absolute best. No matter your lot, your age, or circumstance, the beauty of your character, too, will remain.

You have to count on living every day in a way that you believe will make you feel good about yourself, so that if it were over tomorrow, you'd be satisfied... Don't think of all the misery, but of all the beauty that still remains.

Your inner beauty was created by the same God that made the earth. His divine hand brought forth the crystal pure waters, the petals of the flowers and breathtaking sunsets. Open your eyes to God's beauty and to your own.

You are made beautiful by the way you think, act and how you treat your fellow human beings. Your kindest impulse, most generous gestures and loving words, when put into practice will make you radiant! "Man looketh on the outward appearance, but the Lord looketh on the heart." –Samuel 16:7. God judges, not on your outward appearance, but deep within a caring heart and so does any person who judges wisely. What you have in your heart comes to the surface. Do not judge a person on their looks, but on how they act and react to certain situations.

Comfort those in need. Helping others gives you better emotional and physical health. "I am a volunteer for the Cancer Unit at a Hospital," says a local woman. "I have met so many wonderful people and have learned so much wisdom from them," she says. "The patients are appreciative, tolerant and lovely because their circumstances have made them aware of the true beauty that comes from within."

To obtain this inner beauty, talk with God, cherish life's little moments, take a stroll in the park, sip tea with a friend, or laugh with the children. Slow down. These occasions catch the essence of life and that quality time is what makes life worth living.

Clothe yourself in peace and serenity. Be aware of the small pleasures of life and the satisfaction of goals achieved. No need to compare yourself with others; Renoir's masterpieces are incomparable and so are you.

What makes a person beautiful, regardless of their size, shape or color, is their attitude and spirit. Inner beauty knows no boundaries. Your true beauty, like Renoir's painting, is timeless and becomes more valuable with age. Let sorrows and pain be forgotten. The greatest masterpiece on earth is the beauty of your soul. This beauty remains...

Time, Precious Time

"Every second is a new opportunity to live a better way."

Sometimes, as I close my eyes to pray… for that one, brief, glorious moment, time seems to stand still and the peace of eternity breaks on my soul.

Time, our most precious asset. And each year is an added treasure. How can we hold on to our most valued commodity, making the most of the time we have, while not wasting a second?

One of the answers, I believe, is in the words of a dear friend of mine who said, "Time is relative to our obedience to God. He can stretch it, as we obey His will." The value of time isn't in how many years we have on earth, but in what we do with our years.

By putting God first in our lives, and walking with Him according to His plan, we are living a life that is full of purpose. He can take a second and turn it into eternity.

Make having a close relationship with Him a priority. Set time aside to be alone to express your own thoughts and feelings. Take just five minutes to pray and ask God to expand your hours. As you go about your day, if a worry or problem arises, stop for a moment and think, "Father, is this the right thing to do?" Then, leave the issue in His hands. Hour by hour you will feel relieved, loved, and protected.

Take a moment before every meal to say "thank you" for the food on the table. My husband and I hold hands and pray together before we go off to work. Things always turn out better when we begin our day with prayer and thanksgiving.

Live each day as if your life had just begun. There are no dress rehearsals for life. Time is so precious; consider it a gift.

Cherish this moment. Every second is a new opportunity to live a better way. When do you start? The time is now.

Do not be careless. Spend your minutes wisely. When you are tempted to speed recklessly, remember this advice from a reader. "Go slow; take your time. It is better to loose one minute in your life, than to loose a life in one minute." You create your future by what you do in this day. The best preparation for tomorrow is the right use of today.

You will find out that God knows how busy and rushed you are. But know that you can have enough time for all you have to do by reading Ecclesiates 3:1-8. "There is a time for everything, a season for every activity under heaven: a time to be born and a time to die, a time to plant and a time to uproot, a time to wound and a time to heal, a time to tear down and a time to build, a time to weep and a time to laugh, a time to mourn and a time to dance, a time to scatter stones and a time to gather them, a time to embrace time and a time to refrain, a time to search and a time to give up, a time to keep and a time to throw away, a time to tear and a time to mend, a time to be silent and a time to speak, a time to love and a time to hate, a time for war and a time for peace."

Make every moment with your loved ones a time of sparkling joy. Take time to look deep into the eyes of love, to embrace the beauty all around you, and for singing and laughter. Take time to heal… and if you yield to Him your trust and obedience, Ecclesiastes 3:11 says, "He has made everything beautiful in His time."

Eliminate Problems

"Turn your stumbling blocks into stepping stones..."

In one of Aesop's fables, a wise farmer asked his two sons to gather a bundle of sticks. After the boys collected them, the farmer tied the bundles together with a strong, thick cord. "Try to break the bundle," the farmer asked his sons. Each of the boys tried and tried to break the bundle of sticks, but could not do so. "Now," said the father, "Untie the cord and break each stick separately." The two sons did as their father instructed and had no trouble breaking the sticks at all.

This is a lesson we all need to learn, my dear friends. When we are faced with seemingly big and tough issues, break the problems up into small, tiny little ones and thus eliminate them one by one. If you look long and hard enough at a situation, you can turn adversity into a victory.

Life is about trials. Expect these tribulations as an inevitable part of life and when they come, hold your head high, be firm in faith and stronger than any problem can be. Do not let struggles defeat you or keep you from achieving your goals. It's the rough road that leads you to the heights of greatness. Turn your stumbling blocks into stepping stones; to every disadvantage there is a corresponding advantage.

And we've all heard the saying, "when the going gets tough the tough get going!" By looking at obstacles as challenges and putting your whole heart and soul into meeting them, you can overcome just about anything.

"In the middle of difficulty lies opportunity," said Albert Einstein, "from out of discord, find harmony." People who have succeeded in a big way have done so by breaking problems apart. When the Lord wants to give you something of great value, most of the time he buries it in the heart of a problem, then sits back and watches how you will act concerning it. Your reaction determines your future. Success begins with a person's will and in their state of mind. No matter what the issue may be you can conquer it with a positive attitude toward that situation. "The things that hurt instruct," Benjamin Franklin once said. Remember, a diamond has to be cut into many facets before the glory of its character can be reflected.

You can become a better and more successful individual each time you meet a problem head on. Don't dwell on mistakes or setbacks. Learn from them and move on. R.H. Macy failed seven times before his New York store became a success and Walt Disney went bankrupt several times before he built Disneyland. These individuals turned their failures into success!

Give your problems, your cares and your worries to the Lord. His loving eyes are upon you and His arms are around you. "God is our refuge and strength, a very present help in trouble." –Psalm 46:1. Then, step by step, one by one, mold and shape your problem into something beautiful… giving you the victory.

Second Chance

"Aim high, for the aim if reached this year or next, makes life great."

There is something so wonderful about being given a "second chance." An opportunity to start again, to begin fresh and anew with a clean slate. An exciting new adventure to once again try to tackle, an occasion to achieve a dream left behind or an instance to mend a wrongdoing.

The Lord, in all of His mercy and goodness, always grants to us the grace to try again. A second chance to conquer and win, with all the wisdom learned from past experiences. What would you do over again? How would you change your life? This is a time of new beginnings. Now is the second chance to heal broken relationships, to start fresh with love, determination and prayer.

Find confidence within your heart and let it guide you to strive for your innermost and beautiful dreams and goals. "He did it with all his heart, and prospered." –2 Chronicles 31:21. What you set your heart upon surely will be yours. Henry David Thoreau wrote, "I learned this, at least, by my experiment: that if one advances confidently in the direction of his or her dreams, and endeavors to live the life which they have imagined, they will meet with a success unexpected in common hours."

Persistence, to me, is a great word. Nothing in the world can ever, ever take the place of persistence. If you keep on going, keep on trying, again and again, chances are you will meet success. The journey of a thousand miles begins with one single step. So, little by little and inch by inch, closer to your goal you will be… as long as you don't give up! Like a reader who wrote, "At the age of 33, I am pursuing my life long dream of becoming a physical therapist."

Build on faith rather than doubt. See the endless possibilities that are ahead. There is no limit on what you can accomplish, no ambition too large and no dream too far. It all starts with the right attitude. Nothing can stop the person from achieving his our her true desire if they begin with, and continue to keep, a positive frame of mind. Pray for the Lord's will in all of your endeavors. In all ways acknowledge Him and He will direct you toward success. "In his heart a man plans his course, but the Lord determines his steps." –Proverbs 16:9.

Leave the past behind. You can't change history, so learn from the events of the past and then move on. If you spend your precious time fretting about what might have been or what could happen you can loose the joy and wonder that only this sweet day can bring. Do not worry, God's grace is new each morning.

We all have been given a second chance. This year holds for us, dear readers, a new and exciting chapter in our lives. Write down, today, a detailed list of your own special hopes, plans and dreams for the future. Aim high, for the aim if reached this year or next, makes life great.

With unflinching steadiness, march on your path believing that you have a loving Father who will be your guide, your helper. And He is the giver of all that is good and beneficial for your life. When you turn to Him, make Him your partner and He will pour new life into your being. All things will become fresh and new and you will succeed.

You're Special in God's sight

"The deepest principle of human nature is the craving to be appreciated and the desire to be important."

I remember, years ago asking my mother, "Of all of your five children…which one of us do you love the most?" She thought for a moment, as a tear of love came to her eye. With compassion in her voice she said, "My darling daughter, I have five fingers on my hand…I could not do without any of them; each one is important, unique and special… I love you all."

We all want to feel as though we are here for a special reason. American Philosopher William James wrote, "The deepest principle of human nature is the craving to be appreciated and the desire to be important."

Treat everyone that you meet as if they had an invisible sign on their heart that says, "I need to know you appreciate me." Then, respond to that sign immediately. People will react positively to you if they are made to feel important, respected and needed. Recognition and attention are motivaters for happiness and success. By making others feel worthy, just think of what wonderful relationships you could build. Be open to other people's needs, coworkers, spouses, neighbors, bosses, clients and even strangers. Share and spread love and good will and you will receive it back one hundred fold! Let your actions deliver the message, "I care about you."

In business, create a family-type atmosphere and let warmth permeate your company. A friendly, "good morning" or "you have done a great job" can do wonders. Write thank you notes to people who have touched your life in a kind way. That personal touch can work wonders. At home, express aloud how much your loved ones mean to you. "I think you're a wonderful wife" or "thank you honey for your hard work and support" can strengthen bonds to last a lifetime. "My husband and I have been married for 25 years, and the secret to a wonderful life together is to always love and cherish each other ," says a reader. A sincere compliment, giving of your time and loving actions will make those around you feel as if they are special.

Live your life by the golden rule, "Treat others as you would like them to treat you."

A friend of mine always wanted to wear a button that said, "Smile when you talk to me, I'm paranoid." We are not mind readers, if we just see a smile, we will know we are appreciated. The world is like a mirror, it reflects back to you what you express.

You are a child of God, so sweet and precious. No one else is exactly like you. You have so much to offer and must believe in the purpose and capacity that God created you to fill. God delights in you and has miraculous plans for your life filled with happiness, joy and beauty. Put His gifts into action and bring forth the goodness He planned for you.

Love yourself so much that you protect your mind from depression or despair. The Lord loves you and wants you to know you are valuable, esteemed and highly regarded in His sight. You are significant and your place, no one else can take. You're destined for great things.

Dear readers, a mother's heart is the closest thing to God's love. He can not do without any one of you.

God Watches Over Children on Their Own

"There comes a time when we have to let children go out on their own. Parents, do not worry. God will keep His eye on them."

It is September, summer vacations are over and the children are going back to school. Three years ago, my nephew, Michael left home to go to college in Maryland. Seeing his bare room, books and clothes packed up in boxes, was almost too much for me to bear. The thought of not seeing "my boy" on a regular basis filled me with emptiness. "How could this be?" I thought. "Time has gone by so quickly... How did he grow up so fast?" The little boy that I cared for, nurtured and loved, now a young man ready to go off to college, to begin a new phase of his life. What could I say? What advise could I give him? How could I keep him from harm? Tears flowed freely as we said our goodbyes, and a part of me surely went with him.

This month, two more of my nephews, Steven and Billy, are on their way to college. Memories now flood into my mind and I am hardly able to write this, without tears streaming down my face and onto the paper. Looking back at photo albums, I reflect on events that have shaped our lives that hold priceless memories. How can I now prepare them for what lies ahead?

As the children go back to school and the young adults off to college, parents, relatives and friends alike, hope that these precious ones will take with them the years of instruction, guidance and love that we have tried to instill. For along with them... they will carry a part of our hearts.

Parenting is an awesome responsibility. Guiding your child wisely from adolescence to adulthood requires unselfish, active parental involvement. Children are a gift from God, the richest of all blessings. Each child is an individual jewel and should be encouraged to become his or her own wonderful self. Do not attempt to mold him into the image of another, each child is unique.

Your child will learn from watching you. Children will reflect your life just as a mirror reflects an image. Set the example that you want those you love to follow. Reinforce family values. Set the rules. Teach children to respect other's property and privacy. Instruct them to tell the truth and to keep their word.

Build a child's self-esteem. Tell them over and over that they are precious. Use caring words and gestures. Demonstrate love. When a child feels love and affection they can accomplish great things.

Encourage children to be kind, to treat visitors with courtesy and to be considerate of the elderly. Children who help others feel good about themselves and those who are busy doing "good projects" are less likely to have time for destructive ones.

Teach children to work hard. Allow them to follow their own special dreams, no matter how far-fetched they seem. If their calling is performed with a brush, a shovel or a surgical instrument, let the child know that a purposeful life is a rewarding one. Work is not a bad word. Hard work can be gratifying and a pleasure.

Do not worry about protecting your child from every disappointment. Adversity strengthens character and makes us compassionate. Your child is bound to have some trouble in his or her life, so let them learn now how to handle it wisely. Teach them to love God and to pray. For faith can give the strength a child needs.

There comes a time when we have to let children go out on their own. Parents, do not worry. God will keep His eye on them. The bonds that we created, woven in love, can not be separated by time nor distance. Love is the strongest force in the world. It is a tie that binds us together for life.

From my heart to yours... may God be with the children.

Healthy Eating

"Get your body in harmony with regular exercise, nourish your soul with prayer and meditation, and eat wholesome food when you're hungry and drink pure water when you thirst."

Eating is meant to be one of life's grand pleasures. Preparing a meal, setting a beautiful table and enjoying the company of good friends can be a wonderful experience. In order to live, our bodies need food, the source of fuel needed to be converted into energy. But for many, food is their enemy, shortening lives, making them prone to indigestion, obesity, and heart attacks. Respect the healthy laws of nature and fulfill that need to indulge by eating food that is both nutritious and appealing. So break the yo-yo dieting syndrome and lets use a common sense approach to weight loss. Get your body in harmony with regular exercise, nourish your soul with prayer and meditation, and eat wholesome food when you're hungry and drink pure water when you thirst. Thank the Lord that we have these choices within our reach…for many do not.

- Self-respect will help you possess a positive body image and you will see pounds melt away. That is one of the only weight-loss tools you'll ever need.
- Fit regular exercise into your day. It is one of the single most important things you can do for yourself. Exercise will strengthen the heart muscle. It's life enhancing. Keep your body moving! It may be walking, tennis, swimming, or bike riding. But thirty minutes of aerobic activities such as these, at least three times a week, can restore energy to a listless life.
- Eat breakfast like a king, lunch like a queen and dinner like a pauper.
- Before reaching for a snack, take one minute to focus on why you're eating. Are you physically hungry or perhaps you are just bored or anxious. Try taking a walk around the block instead to help you relax. Then, reach for a piece of fruit or raw vegetables with a fat-free dip.
- When going out to dinner with your spouse or a close friend, order one entree and two salads. Split the entree and save half of the calories. Plus, it is fun to share. Choose lean meats or poultry and plenty of vegetables.
- Drink plenty of water. It helps your body expel toxic chemicals and metabolizes fat. Water is the secret to good health and weight loss. Experts recommend eight ounces a day.
- For a quick and easy lunch or a light dinner, buy packages of pre made salad ingredients. Just cut open and serve with a lite dressing or balsamic vinegar. Add slices of egg, grilled chicken or a cup of tuna for a healthy alternative.
- Schedule classes, do gardening and other distracting activities for the times when the cookie jar calls out.
- Use positive images. Visualize how you will look and feel once you begin that exercise program or have lost those five pounds.
- Reduce temptations. Try brushing your teeth after eating to avoid picking and snacking.

- "I lost 40 pounds by cutting the fat in my diet," says a reader. "Now I buy fat-free snacks, low-fat cheeses and fresh fruits. I feel great and have so much more energy."
- Limit your sodium intake. Check food labels and avoid salty foods.
- Use lemon juice, herbs and spices in place of salt in recipes.
- Consume lots of dark green leafy vegetables like spinach, which has few calories and lots of calcium. Increase your fiber intake by eating whole fruits and veggies rather than drinking their juices.
- Trick your chocolate craving. Have a glass of skim milk with a heaping teaspoon of Nestle quick.

It helps to have someone who cares to share in your frustration of slow weight loss and to rejoice with when the 20, 30 or more pounds come off. So, dear readers, I am here with you and for you. To glory in your success and encourage you through your setbacks. These tips I'll be using too. So together we can live a full, healthy, happy and balanced life.

* Be sure to check with your doctor before beginning any diet or fitness program.

Love is a Treasure You Work to Keep

"Real love and caring is shown when the hard times come."

In this small space in time, among the millions of people on earth, through far and distance lands…how incredible and miraculous that you and your mate could have found each other. God's plan.

Gathered together, in the sight of God, a man and a woman are joined as one in Holy Matrimony. Two lives and two hearts united. "For this cause shall a man leave his father and mother and shall be joined unto his wife and they two shall be one flesh." –Ephesians 5:31.

To have and to hold, for better for worst, for richer for poorer, in sickness and in health, to love and to cherish… as a ring is gently placed on your beloved's finger, the unbroken circle of the wedding band represents eternity. A circle of love that has no end. Bound together for life in a relationship that will profoundly influence your entire future, a lifetime of hopes, disappointments, successes and failures, pleasures and pains, joys and sorrows. These elements are mingled in everyone's life, here on earth, and are to be expected in your own. However, if you can stick together lovingly, faithfully and upholding each other through all of these contrasts, the sweet and the bitter, then you have acquired two of the most valuable treasures on earth…a noble and beautiful character and a lasting marriage. "We accept the bad with the good," states a couple who have been married for 55 years. "Struggling together made us better people, stronger and closer in our relationship."

Anything of great value is difficult to attain, like gold and diamonds which are mined from out of the deep earth. Life can bring tears and suffering, but together through love, you can overcome any adversity and persevere. Be patient in times of trouble. It isn't always easy, but love conquers everything. Real love and caring is shown when the hard times come. Be kind, sympathetic and let your love comfort each other like the warm sun after a cold storm. A soft touch, kind words in open communication can sustain you even through the most difficult day.

Enjoy every minute of your marriage, God will bless and guide you in the pathways you both follow. Celebrate the joy of being together. Share verbally with each other the things that make you happy and thankful. Keep God in the center of your relationship. Your life and your love is in His hands. With God, you will have a strength that cannot be broken, a beauty that can't be described and a joy that is unsurpassed. Love is God and eternal, the most powerful force in the world.

Married love need not diminish with accumulating years. The sparkle of romance need not leave the relationship. Treat your husband or wife of 5, 15 or 50 years like a newlywed. You work hard at your career, your home, your garden; work at your marriage and love will grow through the years. Sometimes, the romance of love seems to have flown away for a bit, but with patience and kindness, as sure as the sun rises in the east, romance will return again and the sunrise will bring much more joy, love and happy times.

Cling to your promises and vows of love. Pledge a rekindled faith in each other and renewed respect for the person you married. Your marriage vows are still very serious, sacred and freshly spoken in God's sight. For He dwells in eternity where no time has passed since you said them.

The Law of Contrasts

"Rain comes with cloudy overcast days, but how precious those rainy days are to the little thirsty growing flowers, grass and trees."

You've heard the saying, "Into each life a little rain must fall." It is a part of the law of contrasts.

What if you planted a lovely garden. Delicate lilies of the valley, fragrant hyacinth and blooming azaleas lined your walkway. Tulips in an array of gorgeous colors. Picture perfect crocuses. Bright yellow daffodils which have been called nature's most cheerful flowers that whisper "spring is here" to passersby.

And, what if, every day of the spring and summer season, the weather was warm, the sunshine was brilliant and the blue sky clear without a hint of a cloud. From April to September without a drop of rain. Suddenly you noticed everything in your garden had shriveled up.

Rain comes with cloudy overcast days, but how precious those rainy days are to the little thirsty growing flowers, grass and trees.

Our lives, too, would become dried up and dull if we didn't have the contrasts that keep us enjoying the good things. As Helen Steiner Rice wrote, "God did not promise sun without rain, joy without sorrow or peace without pain." But He will give us strength in these contrasts, "Help from above, rest when we are weary and undying love."

Along with the many blessings must come trials. Why do we sometimes have to experience adverse times? Because God's ultimate goal is to see you triumph over adversity. When we overcome difficulties, we experience greater freedom, wisdom and a power within. Our true character is revealed when we are tested. God allows trials so that we can be aware of that which is good, peaceful and strong.

After six days of a hurried business week, meetings, phone calls, deadlines and rush hour traffic, how wonderful a day of rest is – time to call your own. Another prime example of the law of contrasts.

God is all wise and He knows that all things work together for the good. No matter what we may be suffering from right now, the difficulties or discouragements, He will give us a long, glorious day that will be made for unspeakable joy… because it is such a contrast from the pain we have gone through. It is a fight to have the right attitude to endure these things. But when you do, you know you are gaining much more through your suffering.

Pray continually for strength and for a sense of humor to keep life from overwhelming you. Laughter can break the strain and stress. The Bible says, "Laughter is medicine for the bones." Therefore, laughter is healing.

Life keeps demanding that you grow. For with adversity comes the challenge to achieve wisdom, compassion and understanding.

How beautiful and comforting are the words, "I know how you feel," or "I have been through the exact same thing." God, who is so precious, always gives us someone to help us through trying times. When we suffer we grow also. "Blessed is the man who perseveres under trial, because when he has stood the test, he will receive the crown of life that God has promised to those who love Him." –James 1:12. It is the law of contrasts.

Don't be discouraged. Keep loving God no matter the disappointment, for He said, "For I know the plans I have for you, plans to prosper you not harm you, plans to give you hope and a future. Then you will call upon me and come and pray to me and I will listen to you. You will seek me and find me when you seek me with your whole heart."

Amazing Grace

"Whether in the heights of happiness or the depths of despair God is forever there."

John Newton was a slave trader who almost lost his soul in the search for power, money and pleasure, and adopted a life of immorality and crime. An expert seaman, he became captain of his own slave ship at the age of 23. His life was abominably wicked and vile.

One night, during a raging storm at sea, Newton feared for his life. When all seemed to be over for him and his crew, he cried out to God for help. Miraculously, the storm was stilled and his life was spared. From that point on, Newton renounced slaving, left the sea and spent the next 16 years preparing for the ministry. God's grace came into his heart and his life changed completely. Thereafter, because of this transformation, while he was a pastor of a parish in Olney England, John Newton wrote his tribute to the loving God who had saved him.... The song he wrote was "Amazing grace!"

"Amazing grace! How sweet the sound, that saved a wretch like me... I once was lost but now I'm found, was blind but now I see." This lovely hymn touches the spirit of millions throughout the world and has a special anointing upon it. Since Newton's "moment of grace" during the life threatening storm, he was able to see the light of God's love, kindness and compassion transforming one of the worst examples of humanity, his own self.

In the presence of God, we too, can find this incredible joy, love, peace and amazing grace. "You have made known to me the paths of life; You will fill me with joy in Your presence." –Acts 2:28.

See God in the gentle rain that nourishes the thirsty flowers, in the laughter of children at play and in the stillness of the night as one tiny star lights the way. Look for Him in all creation, but mostly see Him deep within your own surrendered and humble heart.

I cannot express in words the wonderful, satisfying joy that comes from loving the Lord. When I'm a bit down, His words fill my heart with peace, when I need comfort His promises give my soul inspiration and when I'm helpless His word gives me strength. "The Lord is my rock, and my fortress, and my deliverer; my God, my strength, in whom I will trust." –Psalm 18:2. Line yourself up with His word. Sometimes we all get so busy with careers, families, chores and so on, we forget Him, and God seems to say, "I love you," "I miss you," "talk to me," "pray to me," "remember me." Instantly, when we include Him in our daily lives, a happiness washes over our entire being and we walk above the cares of the world.

Whether in the heights of happiness or the depths of despair God is forever there. We must go to Him. Do you ever wonder why you are passing through these special trials? There is a reason for each heartache, though we cannot see it now. Wait a little longer and you will share with others God's antidote applied and know why you were afflicted.

Maybe we must go through these trying times so that we can be a comforter to others. "I know how you feel," "I can help you," can be like waves of healing truth to the recipients ears. Remember, God is no respecter of persons; what He has done for others He will do for you. If you call on Him, with the sincerity that they had, He will deliver you also.

As with the author of "Amazing Grace," God can change your life. Nothing can separate us from the love of God and if that love is preeminent in any relationship you'll always be together. Let His divine love be the motivation for your every thought, attitude and action and you will find it's a wonderful new life.

The Quiet Center

"Eavesdrop on the melody's of the earth, the sound of the squirrels, the birds and the rippling brook."

As the twilight descends on us ever so early, Autumn has returned. The hills and valleys are clothed in pure gold and the mountainside is burnished with orange and maroon. The smell of roasted chestnuts, old-fashioned apple pie and warm cider filters the air, charming us once again with the good things of life.

Refresh your spirit and fill your soul with appreciation for these precious days and shining hours.

Whenever you fall prey to the stress that life sometimes sends your way, head to a quiet place, a gentle retreat, to be restored, renewed and rejuvenated. Artists know the treasures of having time alone. They become one with nature. You also should try a walk in the country or the park and inhale the beauty that surrounds you. Eavesdrop on the melodies of the earth, the sound of the squirrels, the birds and the rippling brook. Let your cares and worries pass by as you seek comfort and peace in the wondrous symphony of creation. "Last week I took some short trips by myself in which I drove in or through five of our beautiful New England states," wrote a reader. "Throughout my time away I realized how beautiful our country really is and how fortunate we are to live in a land of peace and freedom." Spending time alone with your own thoughts can help you to appreciate and focus on the many blessings you have in your lives. Present yourself with an hour, a morning or a day just for your own reflection and enjoyment. Let your mind dwell on the loveliness and splendor around you. The gift of quiet time to think and see as a child again can be utter bliss. Solitude is a lovely word and every so often it is important to tend to your own thoughts that need pursuing, to dream new dreams and to discover the wondrously soothing and healing balm of nature.

Here are some suggestions to help you to find the quiet center of your life, to forget the negative and focus only on the positive.

- Open up an absorbing book of inspiration and read. Abraham Lincoln said, "My best friend is a person who will give me a book I have not read." Longfellow wrote, "Lives of great men all remind us we can make our lives sublime."
- Start a journal with lovely memories that will rekindle thoughts of thanksgiving for yesteryear. Every wonderful coincidence is really the hand of God in your life.
- Listen to soft music to wind down and relax. If we are tense this can be very therapeutic.
- Try your skill at painting, gardening or writing. By creating something in which you can express your thoughts and feelings, you can discover what a truly special and unique person you are.
- After working all day, unwind by taking a dance class. Exercise can help you to unwind and eases tension.
- Write a letter to a long distance friend or a poem to your spouse. These things take time and are seldom done because of the hours involved. But they are such a treasure to the recipient...like your letters are to me.

Most of all, in the quiet center of your life, talk to God. He never turns away His sincere and appreciative children. A longing to share your joys and bless your days with love, is at the quiet center of His heart.

Loved Ones Live on Forever in Our Hearts

"Those we love are never really gone"

Though some of our loved ones are no longer with us, here on earth, they can still live inside of our hearts and our minds.

Those we love are never really gone. We can experience them in so many ways, by their dynamic personality, through the friends they cared about and the dreams they shared. And the memory of their words can give us strength to face the challenges that lie ahead.

I can still hear my mother's voice ringing in my ear, "I just want you to be happy," she says.

Life is short. Do not waste a passing moment on discouragement. Out of the time we are allotted, we must choose to be happy and to spin from it love, goodwill and eternal friendships.

What will you do and how will you spend your precious time?

You and I have only one life to live. Do what makes you and those you love happy today. Not next month or next year. Do not procrastinate. Do it now. Today is your day. Contribute to it all that you can. Reach out to others. If you can make the most of what you can control in your life each day and make a positive difference to somebody else's life, then that's a great thing.

Have the courage to take action. Do not be afraid. Many a time, when my heart beat the loudest, when my hands shook the most and I wanted to get up and run, that was the time that I stuck it out and in the end found success. You never know what you can do unless you try. Have high hopes, for what you think about and dream of becoming you will become.

Time passed can not be regained. There is no time like the present to take action. Live one day at a time; each second is a unique opportunity. No day repeats itself precisely like the last. In the case of a difficult day, that is good. But, most of our days are good days. Hours full of promise. A single smile brought to someone else's heart is always doubled on its return trip to you. Smiles and sincere compliments are affordable gifts on anyone's budget. Give them freely and watch them return in the wrappings of peace and contentment. God gives to us His love each day. His magnificent love lives on and on. And yours can too.

Whenever I feel down or apprehensive about going after a dream or a goal, my mother's words and the memory of her life forges me onward. I recall how quickly life can be taken away. That knowledge alone is enough to enjoy the present and to live my life, each waking hour, to the fullest. I know, that's the way my mother would have wanted it.

Then, once again, I hear the ringing of her sweet voice in my ear, asking me if I'm o.k. and if I am happy. In a single breath, I feel the words building inside of me and they come to me in a whisper. I say them to her as prayer and as praise. I say, "Yes, Mom I am so happy... Thank you for my life."

In the evening, when I close my eyes to go to sleep, I say a prayer of thanks to God for granting me another precious day.

The Greatest Lesson of All Attitude and Gratitude

"Living your life with gratitude is the only way to have the right attitude to carry you through day after day."

The good Lord sometimes allows me to have a disturbing dream in the night to adjust my attitude, to show me what could be and to help me appreciate all the good things and blessings that I have. For the enemy tries to make me be dissatisfied with the status of my life, as he does to us all.

In the morning, when I awake to calm, to know that everything really is all right, then, the Lord has given me the greatest lesson of all… Appreciation for the design by which He has shaped my life so far. When I start thanking Him for every good thing, then I literally do WAKE UP.

Living your life with gratitude is the only way to have the right attitude to carry you through day after day.

Yes, we are so busy; we have careers, family's and homes to take care of. Yes, there are people who try to get you down, but there are others whose friendship is so valuable and precious. Yes, we have heartaches and trials, but we also have blessings and joys beyond measure. Sometimes you just have to look for them and focus on them. Focus is really just another word for discipline. "I have many things to be grateful for," wrote a reader. "A good husband and sons who help me as much as they can, a home, good health, a car to drive and plenty to eat."

If we leave our mind unguarded then the enemy can put every kind of negative thought into it. It is his job to make us dissatisfied with everything God has given us and every person He has put in our lives. But, I believe every one of us is smart enough to know his tactics and to know how to defeat his darts. "Do not be overcome by evil, but overcome evil with good." –Romans 12:19-21. We must first look on all human beings with eyes of compassion. This was one of Jesus's greatest attributes. He showed us that the quality of a compassionate person is a beautiful one. Isn't it wonderful to read a column that states with understanding just what you have been going through? Compassion and understanding filled with love is healing.

When you wake up in the morning you have to smile… You have 24 brand new hours before you. God gave this present to you. It's only polite to say "thank you" to someone who gives you a gift. Vow to live each hour full of purpose and gratefulness every waking moment and the strength of His love will flow into your life. Be determined to have the right attitude, the attitude of gratitude. God forgives and overlooks all kinds of failures if our attitude to Him is of love, thankfulness and determination to do better each and every day.

Behold the beauty and wonder that surrounds you. Lift the shades of your mind and let the Son shine in. You can view the beautiful outdoors and listen closely to the sounds of nature, the trees rustling, the birds chirping. We have to pull together to get up this road in life. And there are definite directions to reach our destination.

At the end of each day, give yourself time to read the directions how to get to that lovely celestial city written of in the Bible. And talk with the Map Maker to be sure you understand every hidden turn.

I am writing to tell you, dear readers, of the challenges I encounter every day and I'm giving you my secrets of how to overcome, and reach your destination with joy and rejoicing.

To Find Victory Read Bible and Ask, Seek and Knock

"Ask and it will be given to you; Seek and you will find; Knock and the door will be opened to you." –Matthew 7:7

One of my favorite verses in the Bible comes from Matthew 7:7. "Ask and it will be given to you; seek and you will find; knock and the door will be opened to you."

I asked, sought and persistently knocked... Now the door that leads from my heart to yours has been opened. We have been brought together for a reason, you and I, so take a moment now to close your eyes and fold your hands in prayer. Ask God to guide you where He wants you to be and where you can best serve His purpose. With God as your partner, you can make wonderful plans.

There is an infinite power in every cell of your being that allows you to accomplish great things. Joined together with God, the things which at first seemed impossible can become possible. Tap into His resources. Our loving Father never fails to give us what we want, if it is sincerely asked to be used for our good and His glory. Prayer is a method that includes thanking and asking. It allows the Creator's energy to flow through you.

Ask for exactly what you want and check your motives. Be definite and specific. All that you want can come to pass with an unselfish desire to help others. Many people fear rejection. It takes courage to ask for what you want. But please listen carefully. Persist! The more you believe that you will receive, the easier it gets to be strong and courageous.

Seek advice from those you admire. Great people will share their secrets. Have faith in your abilities and work hard. Seek openings by believing that you will succeed in your venture. Belief in yourself will give you the confidence needed to make things happen. If you believe in your heart you can achieve – you will! If you meet a person that needs encouragement, say a kind word to them, lend a helping hand, share a smile or a hug. Many a time, it was, and is a stranger's inspiring word or action that was the motivating factor that helped me to persist. They came like God's angels on earth.

Knock. If you knock long and hard enough at the gate, someone will open the door. Successful people keep at it. Great ideas are worthless unless they are carried out to completion. God helps those who helps themselves. If a door closes, never give up. Keep on knocking and another will open. Press on to victory.

So, my dear readers, ask, seek and knock. Submit to His will. One day, in God's perfect time, He will bestow upon you and guide you to your heart's true desire. And each day, I am thankful to the Lord for guiding me to you.

In the evening, when the golden sun sets, I can hardly wait for morning to come upon us again, to awaken, and begin a new, exciting day. So many possibilities lie ahead, dreams yet to be discovered, love to be shared and wonderful people to meet. It is a beautiful life!

The Root of Bitterness

"Leave all bitterness, malice and strife behind and rejoice over the wonderful things in your life."

The sweetest victories in life come from overcoming hard circumstances. Life is a testing ground. Great beauty is revealed in wisely enduring the trials we go through. That supernatural internal beauty is the character of patience, kindness and persistence.

To live this life victoriously and successfully we must continually keep the root of bitterness out of our hearts. We all have trials, and because of them, we will become either embittered old men and women or we will conquer the root of bitterness with forgiving love.

Some people have let bitterness grow so deep, unable to trust, believe or hope again. But the Word of God is true and it says, as a reader wrote, "'God never gives us more than we can bear' so, no matter the test we must trust Him and never doubt Him." It also says to cast your cares upon Him. That's truly the only way you can bear all things.

You've heard the saying, "Nip it in the bud." If we don't stop the bitterness that wells up within us through the single action of one individual, it becomes like crab grass; it grows and grows – it invades and spoils everything in your life. The Bible says, "The devil walks about like a roaring lion seeking who he can devour." But the rest of the verse says, "Greater is He that is within us than he that is within the world." Look what happens when we give up and get rid of the bitterness… we outsmart the enemy. Let's realize that the trial was only one small incident in our whole life. When we keep it contained to that one small circumstance and pray about it, God will give us the grace to show His love to the person who wronged us. Then we have become mighty conquerors. Do not continue to discuss a negative situation or mention it again. The more you talk about it the more it stays alive. If someone does something to offend you return that evil with good.

"Through your column I have found ways to believe that hardship is not as dark and empty as it once seemed," wrote a reader. "I was feeling bitter and couldn't understand how God could make me suffer and go through this difficult time. But now I know He was testing my strength and my faith and I believe I am a stronger person." Connect with God through prayer. Share your thoughts openly and comfortably with Him. Get so close to God that NOTHING will offend you.

Don't be full of resentment. It will hurt you more than the other person. Let it go and drop it in the sea of forgetfulness. Pray and show overcoming love for it's written, "Love never fails."

Leave all bitterness, malice and strife behind and rejoice over the wonderful things in your life. There are so many. Be like the lovely trees, arms up and outstretched thanking God for every beautiful thing we have.

This great revelation will give you freedom and renew your youth like the eagle. God is in control. Never be upset with Him for what He allows. He has a reason for all that He does and it is to bring out the finest in you. There is reassurance always to be found in our heavenly Father's care.

Dig out the roots of bitterness. Lay the axe to the root of that tree.

Let the handle of that axe read, "Faith in God" and "Restore unto me the joy of the Lord." Swing it and sever that root. When that life sapping tree falls, in its place comes up the Rose of Sharon and lovely lily of the valley.

And up above it, in the soft dawn of the sky, the Bright and Morning Star shines upon the beauty of your soul.

My Labor of Love

"Our lives should represent making the way easier for those with whom we come into contact."

How can I begin to tell you how much your kindness, warmth and love has touched my heart. Words cannot express my gratitude to you, my precious friends and dear readers. Your beautiful letters, encouraging words, little gifts and well wishes mean so much to me. I am truly blessed and genuinely appreciative of you. No one makes it alone...

Two of the most important things I have in my life are a binding relationship with God and the wonderful closeness of genuine friends. I am thankful for the special bond that you and I share. This is not a chance meeting; we have been brought together for a purpose. This reminds me of a blessed story of two brothers.

Back in the 15th Century, Albert and Albrecht Dürer lived in a tiny village near Nuremberg. They were two of a family of 18 children. Both brothers had a dream of becoming great artists. Their family though, was not financially able to send both boys to study. The two brothers worked out a plan. One brother would go to school to study, while the other would support his brother's education laboring in the mines. Then, they would switch places and the other brother would pursue his dream at school.

For the next four years, Albert financed his brother Albrecht's goal of becoming an artist. When the young man returned to the village after his schooling, Albrecht honored his beloved brother for the years of scarifies that enabled him to fulfill his ambition. "Now," he said, "Albert, it is your turn to go to Nuremberg to pursue your dream and I will take care of you." Tears streamed down Albert's pale face as he sobbed, "No brother, it is too late for me, look at what four years of mining has done to my hands." The bones in every finger of Albert's hands had been smashed at least once and he suffered from arthritis.

Hanging in great museums all over the world are Albrecht Dürer's great portraits, masterful sketches, woodcuts and engravings. But none as powerful as the drawing entitled "Praying Hands." Albrecht drew his brother's abused hands, with the palms together and fingers stretched towards the heavens as a tribute of love to his brother's sacrifice. Millions of copies hang in homes today around the world. No one, but no one makes it alone.

We all need each other to love, to influence and to care about. Our lives should represent making the way easier for those with whom we come into contact. Some people take the time to make the world so beautiful! Thank those who have been good to you. Thankfulness is the grateful recognition of past achievements and the activator of blessings yet to come.

So, on this week of Thanksgiving, let us share the spirit of giving as we and our loved ones are gathered together enjoying autumns fruitfulness, fireplaces burning, chestnuts roasting and the aroma of turkey and trimmings in our kitchens. Consider inviting someone that you know lives alone over to share your meal, for sometimes thereby we have entertained angels unaware... Have a glorious thanksgiving and thank you for bringing so much happiness into my life.

God's Hand

"God has proven many a time that He is faithful to His promises."

"I have held many things in my hands and I have lost them all; but whatever I have placed in God's hands, that I still possess." –Martin Luther.

I agree with philanthropist George Muller that life has its share of hardships, losses and disappointments, but I am not in the least tired, because I knew things would not always be easy. For the glory of God and the encouragement of His dear children, I desired to, one by one pass though them, if only others might be benefited by the experiences I have encountered. Hard times endured keep me sensitive to other peoples troubles and sorrows. You cannot teach what you do not know.

The longer we live, the more trials of one kind or another we will have to overcome. But at the same time, we can grow happier and more assured that we are in the hand of God. Therefore, how can we grow tired of carrying on His work? God has proven many a time that He is faithful to His promises.

You have nothing to fear. Place your life, your family, career and future in God's care. He will never steer you wrong. Have trust, as a small child believes in his or her parent, and rest in God who holds you safely in His hands. The pains of yesteryear and the hurts left behind should strengthen us.

Don't anticipate bad things happening. Immediately cancel out any discouraging thought that comes to mind. When you think or talk negative, then you can actually make that situation happen. Whatsoever you say will come to pass, so start now by saying aloud phrases like, "Everything will be all right," or "I will do the best I can." Make yourself a well of pleasant thoughts. Faithful sayings, inspirational reading material and words of wisdom can carry you though trying times. A person is what he or she thinks about. So, think and act hopeful and positively about everything and expect great results.

You do not have to carry your burdens alone. The Bible says, "Cast all your cares upon Him, for He cares for you." Another way to get your mind off of your troubles, is to help someone else with theirs. A Chinese proverb says, "When I dig another out of trouble, the hole from which I lift him is the place where I bury my own." Tell someone how much you appreciate them, give them a smile and encouragement. When we reach out to others, God sees the heart. When you are busy helping another, you won't have time to think about any problems of your own. And you will find you will be a happier person in the process.

Having a friend with whom you can talk and confide in is a great blessing. Everyone needs a comforter if you ever feel you are in a dark valley. There is no need to be lonely or to walk in darkness because God Himself is the greatest comforter. No trial ever needs to be experienced alone; God has assigned a guardian angel to watch over us.

So, with a heart full of faith, let us focus on all of the blessings and opportunities we have been given. And day by day we will be renewed with the awareness of God's presence in our lives. He has great plans for you. The Lord said, "I will not forget you…I have engraved you upon the palms of my hands." –Isaiah 49:15.

Forget the past and take hold of the future

"Every precious day and each new year holds for you and me endless possibilities, great discoveries and hidden joys."

The world turns, the seasons change. The sweet fragrance of spring melds into an entrancing summer's evening. The brilliant colors of fall whisk away and the bare branches of winter lie above the glistening white snow. To everything there is a season.

Every precious day and each new year holds for you and me endless possibilities, great discoveries and hidden joys. When we arise in the morning we are given a unique opportunity to be transformed. Just as the land thaws from the cold of winter and the seeds renew themselves deep in the ground to blossom into beautiful flowers, our lives, too, can begin again. Leave the past behind. This is your chance to start anew.

Life is made up of contrasts, sweet and bitter. The tests of your will and the trials of the heart may be many, but know that for every storm, a promise is given: This, too, shall pass.

Strive to rise above each dark cloud. There are rainbows of hope, peace and love ahead.

Sweep the cobwebs of the past out of your mind. The ability to forget is a virtue. Yesterday is gone, so do not let former blunders cast a shadow over today or cloud your hopes for the future.

If you worry about the past in this new and exciting day, you will suffer former mishaps twice over. Concern yourself with the here and now. Never let a bad experience poison your attitude about yourself, others or your life. "Everything happens for a reason," my mother would say. There is always some inherent good that will come from your trouble. You may not see it right away, but later on, down the road you will know it. Never dwell on the past, always look forward to the future.

We all make mistakes. These mishaps are a way of teaching you the best lessons in life. Never quit. Press on! Problems are normal and a part of life. Your strength will develop from standing up to them, thinking them through and mastering them.

By approaching any problem with faith and a positive frame of mind, you can always derive good from it, no matter the difficulty.

Be grateful for lessons found in adversity, and thank God for the troubles you have escaped. Why be haunted by the past? Will those bad memories help you in this instance? Do not grieve over failure or regret.

If someone says something to hurt or upset you, let it go in one ear and out the other. That evil has no value, and if dwelled upon and magnified, it can do you great harm. Clear this clutter out of your thinking and replace it immediately with positive reflections and visions.

What's past is past. You can do nothing about yesterday, last month or the previous year. But you have the power to do everything toward making today and all of your tomorrows the best they can be.

The new year is around the corner. Who knows what miraculous plans the Lord has in store for us? Count yourself blessed at every chance, and whatever God gives, gratefully accept.

If we spend our time thanking God for the good things in our life, there won't be any time to cry over the bad. Let disappointments of the past vanish into the sunbeams of new dreams. Live in the present and enjoy every waking hour to the fullest.

Remember, God above loves you, and so do I.

The Evidence Around Us

"Let the shores of peace lap healing waves over your mind and find contentment and refreshment in the simple joys of life."

I love nature. All of the splendor and wonder around us is a loving expression of God. His divine beauty of character is revealed through myriad forms of life He has created. Our reaction to the world that He so joyfully made affects our health and inner beauty. Stop for a moment to look at the sky, the flowers and the trees; feel the atmosphere of God's love as He expresses Himself in this living masterpiece.

Man and nature, unseen angels and heavenly messengers, two different dimensions living side by side and intertwined. Isn't God amazing. Look what He put before us to see, feel, smell, taste, and hear. God put nature around us for a reason. It is healing, inspiring and energizing. We need to get ourselves in touch and in tune with the symphony of creation so we can be all that He meant us to be and stay in our right minds. Life can become so intense and stressful; soothe your spirit and take relief from nature. Step into that almost heavenly dimension and suddenly you will begin to become a whole new person. Let the shores of peace lap healing waves over your mind and find contentment and refreshment in the simple joys of life.

Witnessing these innocent pleasures is like looking at God. Watch in wonder how nature continually renews and refreshes itself, and how serenely it accepts the changing seasons from summer to winter. Go outdoors, hike at one of our state parks, take long walks by the shoreline or pick wildflowers along a country road. There are places to pick berries, hunkering down next to the warm, soft earth. The scent of berries in the air and the sweetness of the one you just popped into your mouth while listening to the birds sing can make you feel like a six-year-old again. It's good for the soul!

Hidden in the seemingly common and simple expression of nature is something mysterious and glorious. Reservoirs of wisdom and many of life's lessons are found here, inviting us to look beyond the ordinary and sense the presence of God. He is showing us what He wants us to be like through nature. The trees are standing straight and tall, arms outstretched praising God.

Once in a while, you see a weeping willow, beautiful in its place, showing us that there may be sorrow in our life. But, how many weeping willows do you see in comparison to all the other sturdy and uplifting trees? Not many. Be patient in times of trouble and know that the Bible says, "By sorrow the heart is made better." As the glorious flowers open up to the sun, we must open to God and learn the secrets of His creation. Yield yourself to the thought, "What can this be showing me?" And allow the precious wisdom into your life.

"What do you think it means?" a friend asked as we both gazed in awe at the two tiny newborn baby birds peaking out from the freshly made nest cradled in her front door wreath. God is always speaking to us in nature… the love inside their home even reaches beyond its doors. During the storms, the father bird watches carefully as the mother bird covers the babies with her wings. Soon, morning comes and the sun shines brilliantly through the crystal clear and freshly cleansed atmosphere. The mama bird returns to her nest with the food she gathered for her babies. How tenderly God teaches us, through the birds, not to worry about our life. What we will eat, drink or what we will wear. Look at the birds living in such joyful simplicity, taking wing and soaring above earthly cares, singing their praises to God. If a little girl watched the robins taking care of their nest and babies, she would learn, if she had no other example, how to take care of her own. Nature is nourishment for our souls, peace for our minds and assurance for our hearts created by God who said, "I will supply all of your needs (physically and psychologically) according to my riches and glory."

Constant Reassurement

"Sometimes you feel you can't go on any longer. Hold on, give it a day or two. Soon, things will begin to get better."

"Everything will be all right," "I know how you feel," "Don't worry," "Remember how God brought you through last year and the year before, difficulties you don't even think of anymore."

Comforting words of reassurement to warm, calm and to let you know that this time of confusion will soon pass. These simple phrases, when spoken by a trusted friend or loved one, can console, strengthen and get you through life's difficult moments.

Sometimes you feel you can't go on any longer. Hold on, give it a day or two. Soon, things will begin to get better. If you are experiencing periods of sadness and you don't know why, just wait. Look up, beyond the clouds, to the pure blue sky where the soaring bird's wing. The good Lord spread above us a precious canopy of blue to remind us to have patience in times of trouble. "They that wait upon the Lord shall renew their strength; they shall mount up with wings as eagles; they shall run and not be weary; and they shall walk and not faint." –Isaiah 40:31.

We go through many storms throughout our lives, but always remember that somewhere up ahead, the clouds will clear and the sky will once again be bright, and the sun will glisten down on the petals of the lily in the field. Just as the flowers need rain to grow, sometimes we must bear sorrow for our lives to be enriched and bloom. If we but ask and believe, angels are always at our side to guide us through times of need, according to our Father's direction. Know that there is a heavenly host around you; a divine love that reveals itself through the little things, the simple everyday tasks if done as unto the Lord.

How comforting to know that we have a Father who loves us. That love is steadfast, constant and consistent. We must have a steadfast, constant and consistent awareness of the One who cares for us so. Just this awareness will create miracles.

Nature can teach us a multitude of things. We learn so much from the tiniest creature to the grandest oak. Watch in wonder as the cute and perky squirrels energetically gather their nuts. Instinctively, they know to collect their food and store it up for when the hard times come. We all need to be like them and collect God's happy promises and store them in our hearts for when the difficulties arise. Imitate the oak tree and lift up your arms and praise God. For God in His strength and love inhabits the praises of His people. Every member of God's creation is linked by a common thread. Outside the window I see two soft doves snuggling side by side on a branch. The sound of contented coo's come from both as they are huddled together. The comforting sweetness of the doves reveals to me the importance of being there for our fellow neighbors, friends and loved ones. Cooing happiness for their success, and when times are low, supporting them and raising them up with soft words of love.

If you feel overwhelmed, spend at least ten minutes talking to the Lord. Ask the questions, listen and watch nature for the answers. "In all ways acknowledge Him and He will direct your path." –Proverbs 3:6. God will direct your footsteps to great fulfillment and countless blessings. There is no sweeter joy than a relationship with Him. His love surpasses all other love. He will do for you what you cannot do for yourself.

Give every problem to Him. His constant reassurement is so warm and comforting. Meditate on and hear His voice saying, "I will never leave you or forsake you." He is as close as a heartbeat. Look around you and see His problem solving wisdom in all nature. And like the still waters of the lakes and pools, reflect the greatness of His love.

The Blessing of Friends

"There is a Friend that sticks closer than a brother."

"Your love has given me great joy and encouragement...." –Philemon 1:7.

I awaken with great anticipation this beautiful sunny morning. As I open my eyes, I know it is Saturday and in an hour I will be calling my best friend and mentor. Though she moved almost two thousand miles away two years ago, we talk often and look forward to our Saturday morning chats over a cup of long-distance tea.

I always pray that one day the good Lord will bring her back home, which, someday soon, I know He will.

I am truly blessed and thankful that God sent me someone so precious, so dear, to help me in my day to day life. There is never a time when I talk to her that I don't instantly feel better about whatever situation I may be experiencing at that time. The sound of her voice, her wisdom and caring advice has sustained me through the hardest of times and brings such joy in the best of times. Even though the Lord may take to be with Him, some of our dearest loved ones, He never leaves us alone. He sends us His angels to minister unto us and gives us mothers, sisters and brothers from His great family.

Neither time, nor distance, nor anything can separate the God-like love of a true friendship.

Best friends are treasures, someone you can confide in, trust and lean on. They hear with their hearts not with their intellect. A friend's sunny smile spreads rays of happiness that can brighten even the darkest hours.

True friends want nothing from you except the joy of your friendship and presence. They want to lift you up when you are down and share the mountaintops of their joy with you.

God's Word says, "To have a friend, you must first be one." So go ahead, stick your neck out, in love, and soon it will be wreathed in flowers of thanks.

Provide emotional support for someone. By communicating and by being a good listener you can help them overcome life's daily problems. Friends comfort when difficult situations arise. Be there when someone needs you.

Let your conversations inspire and lift another up above the irritating problems of this world. You might take a walk together, have a beverage at a quaint café or go on a shopping spree. Just calling to say "hi" or a card sent to let them know you are thinking of them can keep the love of being alive ever apparent.

Believe in your friends. Cheer on their successes and encourage their dreams.

Make them feel special. The need of friendship is a universal force.

Treat all that you come into contact with as though they are your special friends. Share, appreciate and laugh with your fellow human beings and make this world a wonderful place to live in.

Pray for your friends and even for total strangers. You never know the impact your prayers will have on their lives. "I pray for guidance as to where my prayers are needed," says a reader. "What a wonderful feeling it is to know you have helped someone you may never know."

When I read your lovely letters, dear readers, I feel so loved, valuable and special. You are my family, my friends. Your words make me want to open up my heart and give joy to every one of you. It's amazing what a wonderful impact positive words written or genuinely spoken from the heart, can do for a person's life. The world really is full of good and kind folks. The Word of God says, "There is a Friend that sticks closer than a brother."

Blessings to you; may your precious days be directed by God's guiding hand and filled with His love.

God's Miracle... Lauren Grace

"Influence the life of a child and you influence the world."

God gave us a tiny angel, straight from Heaven above.

And looking into my sweet child's precious face, I have experienced a love…the overwhelming love of motherhood…and to me this joyous revelation is enough to understand even greater, the depths of a heavenly Father's love for us.

What a beautiful miracle you created, Lord, in our little Lauren Grace. May I be worthy of this precious gift you have bestowed upon me. May you give me the wisdom and the strength to harvest this new life to bring forth much fruit. Help me introduce her to your wondrous beauty and your glorious ways. When there is a conflict, let me cradle her with love, shower her with affection and nurture her to peace. And most importantly to always guide her closer and closer to You.

I watch her as she peacefully sleeps in her bassinet. Only two days old, she has already brought so much joy and love into our home. I don't know how we lived without her. Now, every breath is for her, her care, her happiness and well being.

All children are a blessing. A visible thought of God, a fresh and radiant bud of wonderful possibilities. They look to us for guidance and thrive on our love, wisdom and support. Influence the life of a child and you influence the world.

Embrace the first moments, days and months of your child's life. A father of two recommends, "Read to your newborn, play music and talk to them as much as you can; I believe that 80% of what they are is developed within the first six months of their life."

Parent, grandparent, friend or neighbor, you can be a positive role model for the little ones and help to guide them to a richer, fuller life. A small gesture, a bit of encouragement, a bright smile can give them hope. Set the example for kids to follow. When they see you lending a helping hand, speaking a kind word or giving a hug, you show them the importance of kindness and the power of love. Children learn what they see lived.

As our child rests in my arms – one tiny, unblemished, pure soul – my heart is captured.

I watch her in amazement, sleeping contently and breathing deeply.

She has her fathers blue eyes with feather-soft eyelashes, porcelain skin, and lots of dark brown hair. Though her hands are tiny, they hold within them the future of our happiness and the potential of all her precious dreams. Never have I felt closer to God than now. He knows how helpless we sometimes are and now I know how greatly His love desires to protect us.

No woman is more blessed than I am. Already, this child has begun to bring out in me, the depths of awareness of totally self sacrificing love, how to care for another far above my own self, and showing me the values of God's love. By her presence, our joys are enriched, expanded and Heaven blessed.

To watch her daddy so confidently holding her in his strong arms, determined to protect, provide and guide, my heart overflows with thanksgiving and my love for him doubled. God has given abundantly above all I could ask or think.

More so than ever, I believe that miracles, no matter how inexplicable or unbelievable, are real and can come true. God, thank you for this blessing and may God give you, dear readers, the courage to ask for your hearts desires. For as you honor Him, He will honor you.

About the author

Catherine Galasso-Vigorito is a weekly columnist for the Journal Register Company. Her column appears in various Journal Register Publications throughout the United States.

Catherine represented Connecticut in the Miss U.S.A. Pageant and is an enthusiastic supporter of various charitable organizations.

She has a daily segment on WELI Radio and her television feature, "A New You," has been seen on local TV stations.

This is the authors first book on selected prose from her newspaper columns.

She resides in Connecticut with her husband, Todd and daughter, Lauren Grace.